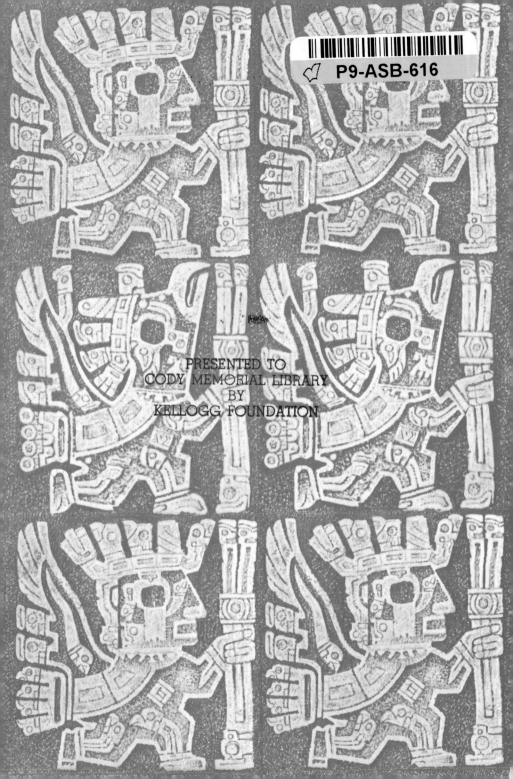

GOLD AND GODS OF PERU
by Hans Baumann

In GOLD AND GODS OF PERU Hans Baumann brings back
to life the fascinating world of the Incas and the other Pre-
Columbian civilizations of Peru. He does so by letting his-
torical sources speak for themselves. They disclose to the
reader the shrouded history of these incredibly advanced so-
cieties, strictly stratified and dominated by powerful gods.

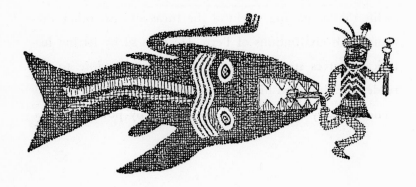

Gold
and Gods
of PERU

BY HANS BAUMANN

Translated by Stella Humphries

Pantheon Books

Contents

Gold and Gods of P E R U

A mysterious word

"Where does Peru begin?" asked a band of Spaniards as they made ready to sail south from Panama more than four hundred years ago, following in the tracks of their fellow countryman Pizarro. It was the question he too had asked before he set out to conquer the kingdom of the Incas. One of Pizarro's sea captains, just back from Peru, had the answer ready. "When you look to the shore and there are no trees to be seen, then you know you have reached Peru."

The Spaniards asked an old Indian as well, and his reply was to take a handful of clay and shape it into a llama. So that was Peru, a land where llamas lived in the mountains, where the shores were bare and no trees grew along the coast. But that was where the Spaniards wanted to go, for they had heard that there was more gold in Peru than anywhere else on earth.

A chieftain's son shook his head at the white men's thirst for gold. "If it is gold you want, if that is why you have left your homes and sailed across the great seas," he told them, "then travel on to the south. There the people bind tree trunks together to make their boats, but their king, the Inca, sits on a golden throne and eats from golden plates. He wears golden robes and he has a house of gold, for the rivers in his realm flow with gold and his subjects bring it to him every day. Go to the land where the Inca rules."

The Spaniards came to the coast where trees were rare and the sand lay thick; where the winds were strong and the bays and inlets gave little shelter for ships. They found rivers whose waters never reached the sea but were diverted to irrigate the narrow valleys which lay between the tracts of yellow desert. The Spaniards made their way into the heart of the land. When they reached the edge of the desert, the mountains rose above them, and presently they found themselves surrounded by volcanoes whose summits were covered with perpetual snow. They had wandered into a world of bare rock, into desolate, empty highlands whose peaks seemed to brush the sky. The men kept seeing ghosts because their lungs could not get sufficient oxygen in the thin mountain air and their vision was blurred. And every day comprised the complete cycle of the seasons of the year. It was spring in the morning, summer at noon, autumn in the evening, and winter at night. Further to the east they were halted by impenetrable primeval jungle.

So this was Peru, a land with three faces: a land of desert, of rock, and of jungle. How can people exist in such a country? marveled the Spaniards.

They could not get over it. For there were people living in places where not a tree, not a bush could grow. There were towns, too, and cities bigger than Toledo. There were magnificent roads, better than those in the Old World. Peru, as a state, was better governed than Spain. Above all, it contained what they were seeking: gold.

Until the Spaniards came, all the gold in Peru belonged to one man, the Inca. Dazzled by such a wealth of precious metal, the *conquistadores* put the Inca to death and all the gold became theirs. Everything which fell into their hands—golden vessels and crowns, idols and masks, ornaments and temple roofs—they melted down into bullion. And when they could discover no more gold in the obvious places, they began to search for hidden gold. They sought it in tombs, in pyramids and temples. They had learned a magic word from the Peruvians: *huaca*. To the Peruvians, the *huacas* were holy places, shrines. For the Spaniards, *huaca* was identical with gold and the value of gold. No other word made their eyes sparkle so.

Before long Peru was completely conquered, and this ruthless rifling of ruined shrines, pyramids, and graves went on for three hundred years. These fortune hunters and looters were called *huaqueros,* the *huaca* searchers. As the years went by, the gold vessels, the masks, and the crowns were no longer melted down, for there were collectors willing to pay high prices for them as they were. Many of them were ready to buy textiles and pottery into the bargain. Anything that had a market price was torn callously from the earth by these treasure seekers. They never disclosed the source of the articles which they offered for sale, and wherever they had been at work they had the earth plowed over to conceal the traces.

It was only about a hundred years ago that people began to arrive in the land of the Incas who were more interested in history than in money, in putting together fragments of pottery rather than melting down gold. They did not do their digging furtively by night and they did not try to conceal what they found. Every crumb of earth had a value and a meaning for these men.

A few decades ago, on a bank of the Chicama River in northern Peru, an American named Junius Bird started excavating a forty-foot heap of rubble to which a Peruvian explorer, Rafael Larco Hoyle, had drawn his attention. This

Cloth fragment. Probably coastal Tiahuanaco

homely-looking midden was called Huaca Prieta, the "dark *huaca*," and no looters had tackled it before Bird, for it did not look very promising at first sight. But Bird went to work, conscientiously dismantling it layer by layer. In doing so, he found evidence that men had settled in this locality more than four thousand years before. He discovered how these early Peruvians had lived and the things they did. When he had finished, the *huaca* lay before him like an open book. Not a page was missing and scholars could read in it a history which had been written centuries before.

The treasure seekers did not do their digging like this. They were more like people who tear valuable books to pieces and sell the single leaves to the highest bidders. And once the pages are scattered to the four winds, the book cannot make sense any more.

The archaeologist removes nothing until he has noted its

exact position. His work proceeds step by step. He asks the same question as Pizarro: Where does Peru begin? And he too penetrates into the very heart of the land, and deeper even than the *conquistadores*. It is in his power to call back to life a world which has been destroyed. He has to make intensive preparations for his expeditions, and he brings to his task much more than the mere physical equipment for excavation. He has studied the findings of his forerunners in the field, and the fragments and splinters which grave robbers and conquerors throw aside as meaningless are eloquent to the scholar. He knows the significance of many Indian words and he has taken the trouble to master Quechua, the language of the Incas, which incidentally is spoken by more people today than it was when the Incas ruled. Above all, the archaeologist knows what the mysterious word *huaca* really conveys.

"The literal meaning of the word is, in fact, the key to all our research," one archaeologist told me. Strictly speaking, it is not one word, but two. *Hua* means "I" and *ca* means "out of which." So *huaca* is, literally, "out of which I (come)." In this sense, it denotes the origin of each tribe or clan. According to Peruvian mythology, when the firstborn of a tribe died he returned to the place of his birth, and there he was transformed into a *huaca* of nonhuman form, such as a jaguar, a stone, a bear, or a condor.

A hundred years ago Raimondi, who has been called the "greatest of all Peruvian archaeologists," and who spent a lifetime exploring his country, was digging at a place called Chavín when he discovered a large green stone. It was the carved figure of a fabulous creature, half man, half beast, a monster intended to strike fear into those who looked at it. In each of its claws it held a scepter which looked as if it were alive. But what struck one most was its tower of heads, one growing out of the other, the personification of the word *huaca*. As one head springs from another, so do the gener-

Raimondi stone

ations reach back through their forefathers to their origin: that was the message of the green stone which Raimondi found.

Archaeologists have established many facts about Peru, including the "Great Lie" of the Incas. For when the Incas founded their kingdom, they impressed on their subjects how mighty they were. "Before we reigned," so they said, "there was no culture worth mentioning. Only through us, the Incas, did the inhabitants become civilized beings, people who built proper houses, who planted corn and lived in peace. Before we came, they were no better than wild beasts."

The Incas employed "wise men" whose job it was to "rethink" past history. Everything which detracted from the glory of the Incas, the Sons of the Sun, was suppressed. The "rethinkers" made up new songs and stories, and all the subject tribes had to learn: "In the beginning of all things was the Sun. The Son of the Sun, the first Inca, created the first kingdom."

The archaeologists were not deceived. They found kingdoms which had flourished before those of the Incas and cities which were older than the Inca towns. With infinite patience, the scholars have removed layer after layer of history, for everyone has left traces—the *huaqueros,* the Spanish conquerors, the Incas, the founders of the ancient cities, and finally, the very first settlers. The earliest remains were always in the deepest strata and covered by so many other layers that the real beginnings of Peru have been brought to light only in recent years. The last chapters in Peru's history were the ones which the archaeologists revealed first, and they concerned the *huaqueros,* those looters for whom the word *huaca* meant simply "gold." That is why their story must be told first.

The great golden fish

Peru has veins of gold. The rivers of the Andes are gold-bearing, and washing for gold took place very early in Peru's history, in such places as Huari, Capac-Urcu, and Camanti, and many others which have the somber ring of the old Indian names.

In 1814, gold miners at Phara were clubbed to death by Indians from the jungle. About the same time, other jungle tribes stormed the smelting works at San Gabán and the gold mines of Tambopata were attacked too. An English goldsmith who lived on the Hill of Camanti was pinned to the wall of his house by Indian arrows. *This gold is not for you and your like. It is for us who have lived in Peru since the country was first inhabited*—this was the unmistakable message of the arrows.

It was thousands of years ago that Peruvian goldsmiths learned how to work gold into ornaments, vessels, and rai-

Gold crown from the Inca period, found in Tumibamba, a palace of the last great Inca, Huayna Capac

ment. Not only did they mask the faces of their dead kings with pure gold; they plated the walls of their temples with it. They went so far as to weave strands of gold among the straw when they thatched the roofs of their temples—that is, until the conquerors came from Spain.

Then much of the gold melted away. It vanished into Spanish saddlebags and Spanish houses and the holds of Spanish ships. And it disappeared into the earth too. Even today, gold objects are dug out of the ground occasionally. A bulldozer scooping out earth for road construction, for instance, may grab a gold vase in its steel teeth. Not so long ago, a boy and a girl lost their way in a maze of subterranean passages not far from Cuzco, the old Inca capital. They emerged at last, too agitated to speak about their adventure; but at the beginning of it, when they still had a few matches, they had stumbled on treasure-trove. The girl came back with a corncob made of gold and the boy had a little golden fish.

Even today, obstinate rumors persist of bigger fish, in particular a great golden one which has so far defied discovery. One such fish, as long as a man's arm and made of solid gold, was dug out of a royal tomb on the coast in 1566. At that time, there were people alive who knew where a similar fish lay buried, but they would not say where. And hunting for this golden prize still goes on even in the middle of the twentieth century.

There grows in Peru an ancient shrub, coca, which had a reputation for magic powers in the old days. There were some *huaqueros* who swore that if you mixed coca with a crumb of the soil in which you were digging and then chewed it, you would be able to "see" the gold in the earth as you dug. The digger had to spit lavishly on the ground and then pour out a generous libation of corn beer so that the spirits

Dancing foxes. Bronze top for a ceremonial mace. Northern Coast   11

Fish pattern from a Chimu vessel

guarding the gold would get drunk. Farmers have been known to work the terraced fields which date back to the days of the Incas, not for the sake of the crops, but so that they can excavate old sites without arousing suspicion. For it is difficult to obtain a permit for excavation today, even if you are an accredited archaeologist. Every permit must be signed by the President of Peru. For a long time, however, areas not under cultivation were considered no man's land by adventurers and travelers, and anyone could try his luck. The museums of many countries testify to the finds that were made, and innumerable private collections too show that an astonishingly large amount of treasure was smuggled out of Peru centuries after the Spanish Conquest.

A certain Colonel La Rosa, for instance, unearthed some priceless treasure in 1870. There were whole groups of gold figures, such as woodcutters chopping down *algarrobo* trees, and a child swinging in a hammock with a fire burning in front of it to keep away a snake. The colonel confessed to the French archaeologist Charles Wiener that he had melted down several thousand gold butterflies weighing only a few milligrams apiece. They were so light that a puff of air would keep them fluttering.

A German archaeologist named Brüning had a desperate race against treasure seekers in the years 1936-37, and he had the luck to find the biggest hoard of gold of the decade. There were gold plaques with human heads emerging from animal bodies, and goblets with a false bottom. Stones were placed in the hollow between the inner and outer surfaces and they made a chinking sound as one drank. There were gold spiders laying pearl eggs, vessels in the shape of a snail's house, a girdle with jaguar heads, and several gold crowns. The masterpiece, however, was a gold knife, used by the priest for making sacrifices. It measured eighteen inches long, weighed over two pounds, and was thickly inlaid with turquoises. The hilt depicted a winged god with a big crown on his head and hummingbirds in flight as ear pendants.

Brüning made his discoveries at Illimo, Zapame, and Batán Grande. At each of these three locations he found shrines, and in Batán Grande alone there were five pyramids hidden away in the *algarrobo* forests through which runs the River Leche. Gold glitters in the sand of the river bed and the pebbles at the bottom are spattered with gold. Today, deep shafts yawn among the bushes on the riverbanks where the looters have been at work. Around about are the remains of canals built at a time before this corner of Peru belonged to the Inca's kingdom. The fields then were not barren as they are now.

Not far from the five pyramids lies a large estate consisting mainly of sugar-cane plantations. A few decades ago, it was the property of a man who had six sons. As long as the old man lived, no one dared to touch the pyramids, particularly the ancient tombs which they contained. But when the old man died, things changed. The sons had heard a great deal about the *huaqueros* and they did not see why they should not try their luck like other people. Their mother raised no objection and they needed the money. So they began to ransack the pyramids, and before long a whole room in their big house was needed to store the loot, for what they used for their own needs hardly counted at all.

They were not the only ones, however, who started to dig.

13

Workmen whom they employed on their estate got wind of these activities and they said to themselves: "Why should they have it all? What about a share for us?" These laborers, so the story went, were led by a man who was well known and greatly feared. He was a doctor and some years before, he had had a professional competitor. The other doctor was Chinese, a hard-working man who was very popular and had many more patients than his rival because he scaled down his fees according to the patient's means. One morning he was found stabbed to death in his own house. Surgical instruments were missing. Since that day, the other doctor was always known as the *matachino*, the killer of the Chinaman, although he was never brought to trial. When it was dark, mysterious figures appeared in the neighborhood and the *matachino* was said to receive them in his house. They were *huaqueros* and they never arrived empty-handed.

Then one feast day, an incident occurred in Batán Grande which created something of a stir.

The men had been drinking heavily, and one of them disappeared into his house and came out again wearing a robe made entirely of gold sequins. The breast was adorned with a sun surrounded by its rays. What with the beer and the magnificence of his discovery, the *huaquero* was thoroughly intoxicated and he began to dance. At first the spectators were spellbound, but then they started to cheer him on and the *huaquero* danced until his legs gave way. The golden sun began to spin and its wearer collapsed on the ground. The rural police, who were drawn to the spot by the noise, saw the reveler lying unconscious on the ground and they whipped off the robe which had once belonged to a priest or a prince. The *huaquero*, greatly sobered, found himself in prison and the Sun of Batán landed in a museum.

Much of the gold of Batán disappeared into the house of the *matachino*, or so the story goes, and this is how it all started. A man arrived there one day when the *matachino* happened to be alone. The stranger, who refused to disclose his name, was carrying an object beneath his poncho; it turned out to be a heavy gold goblet of the most exquisite workmanship, which he was offering for sale. The *matachino* saw at once that it was priceless and he named a figure which the other man accepted. As was the custom, they had a drink to seal the bargain and the drinking went on for several hours until another visitor arrived. He was the captain of the Civil Guard, the chief of the police responsible for security in Batán Grande. As an old friend of the *matachino* he joined the others in a drink, and a couple of hours later the un-known *huaquero* blurted out where he had found the goblet. It had come from one of the five pyramids.

As soon as the stranger had left, the *matachino* and his friend, the police captain, drove off to the estate. The broth-ers, under cross-examination, admitted that they had "found" a few objects and said that they were willing to dig up "something" for the captain and the *matachino*. As a token of their good faith the brothers gave them a few arti-cles to start with.

That night, the brothers found their house surrounded and they were all arrested. The house was searched from top to bottom—by the police chief and the *matachino!* When the six brothers returned after being interrogated, they found their treasure chamber empty. Meanwhile they learned that the police captain had been doing some digging of his own with the Civil Guard to help him!

In spite of all precautions, however, the looting did not remain a secret, and one day a man arrived who put an end to such goings-on. Julio Tello, one of the most outstanding of Peruvian archaeologists, arrived on the spot, armed with authority to take charge of official excavations and to place the treasure in safekeeping. He found gold chains whose links were worked with tiny faces of foxes, owls, and snakes, pouches with demons' faces of beaten gold, such as the

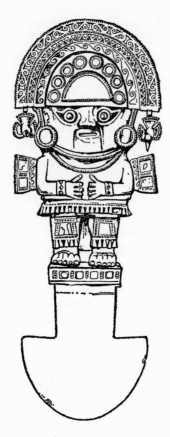

Ceremonial knife. Northern Coast

priests used, and sacrificial knives made of gold and silver rectangles cunningly joined together. There was a priest's mantle made of one thousand six hundred gold disks, and long draperies of beaten gold to hang on the walls of temples. Gloves of gold for the dead were discovered, death masks and scepters, statues of gods, and little golden fishes.

But of the vast golden treasure which the *matachino* had landed in his net, Tello found no trace. Indeed, when Tello began to dig in Batán this sinister figure became his rival. Many of the tombs were robbed at night. Objects which Tello's team had already dug up disappeared. Tello had to put off further excavations until later. But he shot one bolt behind his unscrupulous competitor. He arranged for another chief of police to be appointed in Batán Grande. And before Tello left he made one important discovery. He found a grave in which a priest-king had been buried. The corpse was wrapped in a winding sheet made entirely of thin strips of copper, as green as freshly cut reeds. Among the rich funeral gifts placed by his side were bowls lined with ivory, and engraved on these were mysterious runes. Probably no one will ever decipher them.

Today there are twenty grandchildren of the old man who lived in Batán Grande and not one of them is a *huaquero*. Archaeologists sometimes make them a present of some find or other and these they guard with pride. And since they often receive visits from scholars, they have become more knowledgeable, too, and have learned how to interpret these finds. Just as their grandfather did before them, they keep watch over the pyramids, for they realize how much has been thoughtlessly destroyed already. Once the tombs were decorated with paintings, but none of them are left now.

The *huaqueros* were not fussy about what they removed. They laid their hands on whatever could be sold, or for that matter, on remains which had no value in the market place but which they thought were in the way. Near the entrance to the Cave of the Golden Moon in the Huaroconda Canyon they found a door that could not be opened. It had been so skillfully hewn out of the living rock that it might have been cast in bronze, a door for the gods, to whom solid stone is no obstacle. The treasure seekers were suspicious. They thought that the door was intended as a blind. So they blasted one corner with dynamite; they found nothing but naked rock gaping before them. There was not even a crack in it so that they could probe more deeply. There was no hidden treasure here, so the *huaqueros* withdrew in disgust to ransack some more profitable hoard. But they had wantonly destroyed a masterpiece.

Ever since the sixteenth century, then, when the great golden fish came to light, the *huaqueros* have not stopped dreaming of its counterpart which has never been recovered. The first fish came from the Huaca de Toledo, a ruined pyramid whose Indian name has long been forgotten. It contained treasure worth many millions, and not far away another cache contained gold and silver which weighed the best part of a ton and a half. A certain Escobar Corchuelo and his companions robbed a temple in the Moche Valley and their loot was estimated to be worth twice as much again, not counting articles which they did not declare. These early Spanish *huaqueros* did not dig furtively by night, but went to work openly and boasted about what had fallen into their hands. One-fifth of all the plunder had to be sent as tribute to the King of Spain.

The most daring assault we know of was that carried out by a Spanish captain, Montalva. With a handful of men, he tackled the Sun Pyramid in the Moche Valley, a fortress of a building and the strongest of all the coastal pyramids, with a base sixty-five feet high. When it became clear that it would not yield to conventional methods, Montalva decided to divert the Moche River itself to weaken the temple's foundations. The Indians were forced to dig a new river bed at the foot of the pyramid, and the river, which was swollen by heavy rains from the mountains, tore a breach in the outer shell of the pyramid. Here and there the foundations started to give, the steep walls caved in, and from the rubble the robbers helped themselves to whatever the workmen had not already stolen, including great platters of gold and copper, gold vessels, and a gold statue about a yard high from the girdle upwards and dressed like a bishop.

18

Surprisingly enough, the Moon Pyramid near by was not broken into at the same time. It was excavated much later by an archaeologist named Pío Portugal, and it yielded many valuables: breastplates, brooches, necklaces, bells, spear slings, flutes, fox masks, and diadems. But this was undoubtedly only a fraction of what kings and princes had once deposited inside the pyramid. Most of it has never come to light.

In the early days, when there was no one to guard these sanctuaries, the Indian princes watched the looting going on, and they offered to reveal certain caches to the conquerors. For the Spanish Conquest had so disorganized the economy that the people were in great want and their misery clutched at the hearts of their former rulers. These princes volunteered to tell the Spaniards where they could find hidden gold in return for a promise that the hungry would be fed. In the

Blind door at the Cave of the Golden Moon

year 1550, one prince who had been baptized showed the Spanish leaders the way to Huaca Llomay-huan. The Spaniards, having stripped the shrine of everything they could take, gave nothing in return but their promises. It was years later that they donated 4,200 Spanish talers on behalf of the starving Indians, and in return they expected to be told where more gold was hidden. But by then the prince was not so gullible. Having no power to exchange the concealed treasure for something which would keep the living alive, he allowed the dead to retain the gifts which had been placed in their tombs.

The Chimu chieftain Sacha Huaman offered the Governor of Trujillo objects of incalculable value, including pearl diadems, cushions sewn all over with pearls, chairs with tassels of pearls hanging from the armrests, gold chains, ear ornaments, sandals, and helmets. The gifts were received with smiles, but the smiles vanished as soon as the chieftain began to describe the distress of the natives in moving words. The Governor promised help, but again it remained a promise.

We know of only one Spaniard in those days who did not allow himself to be dazzled by gold. The royal ambassador Pedro de la Gasca, who was sent to put down a revolt and to punish the rebels, returned to Spain with empty hands. Gold was carried down to be loaded onto his ship as he left, but he gave it all away. Everyone else grasped at it greedily.

When the conquistadores first came into Inca country, gold was not hidden, for no one was allowed to own it except the Inca, because he was the regent for the Sun God who traveled across the sky every day.

One of the Spaniards who came with Pizarro to the Inca's capital was an officer named Sierra de Leguisamo. His share of loot was an enormous gold disk, bigger than a cart wheel, the image of the sun. The officer was quite carried away by such unparalleled good fortune and he stayed up all night

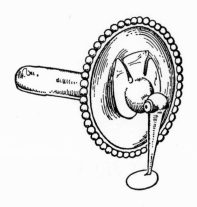

Golden ear ornament. Northern Coast

playing dice, until finally he staked his golden sun on a throw. The dice fell; Sierra de Leguisamo lost. So before the sun had risen, he had gambled it away.

The Spaniard bore his loss with fortitude. After all, they were only a few hundred adventurers to whom the richest land in the world had fallen as prize. With no effort at all, they had captured a kingdom almost four times the size of Spain. They had heard of Peru and its gold and so they went there and took possession of it as confidently as if it had been created especially for them.

They have left indelible footprints in the soil of Peru and many of their tracks can be traced from the first step to the last, even those of the youngest member of their company. He did not see the adventure through Spanish eyes, although he had a Spanish name, Felipillo. The men called him Lenguilla, "Little Tongue," for he was their interpreter. And when the last hour struck for the reigning Inca, it was "Little Tongue" who tipped the scales against him.

Felipillo's story

I came with them. I was there from the beginning when the Spaniards conquered Peru. I helped Pizarro so that the victory was his and not the Inca's. Perhaps I, who wore no sword, contributed more to the Conquest than many of the officers and foot soldiers. For I had one advantage over all the Spaniards. I had been in Peru before.

Who was I? An Indian boy. What was my name? I cast my real name, my Indian name, as a snake sloughs its skin. I slipped into the new name which the Spaniards gave me when they baptized me. I was thirteen then, and from that day on I was called Felipillo. It was Pizarro's field chaplain, Father Valverde, who christened me. He, too, was responsible in great measure for the fall of the Inca Atahualpa. In one hand he held a crucifix and in the other, the book they call the Bible.

But first let me tell you about myself and how I became Felipillo.

I was traveling with some merchants who had taken me

with them on their long voyage because I showed them that I was eager to go and, being an orphan, had no one to hold me back. We sailed along on a balsa raft, a company consisting of two merchants who were very finely dressed, ten other men, four women, and me. We had many kinds of goods to sell: cloth and vessels of gold and silver, scales with carved beams and nets of mesh hanging from each end, and much besides. It was a big raft and the sail was even wider than the raft itself. We made good progress, for the wind was blowing from the point where the sun stands at noon. In the morning the sun rose from the coast, and in the evening it sank into the sea. We were going northward, as I learned afterward from the Spaniards.

It was on the thirteenth day that we met them. First we saw a sail, and then a great house which moved steadily across the water. Later I was told that a house like this with sails is called a ship. As it came toward us, we looked up and saw men outlined against the sky. Their faces were paler than ours and they all wore beards like Viracocha, the old god whom we worshipped. At first we thought that they must be gods too, or the sons of gods at least, for once upon a time, so it had been said, Viracocha, the bearded god, had sailed away across the sea, promising that he would return when the time was ripe. Now the day had come, we thought, and we were afraid.

But the sons of the gods were friendly. They climbed down onto our raft and looked at the goods we were carrying with us. What interested them above all were the objects made of gold. They spoke to us, but we did not understand them and presently we dared to ask them if they were the sons of Viracocha. Then they laughed, for they did not understand us either, but they fetched two Indians from their ship and we could understand something of what they said. The Indians told us that these white men had come from far away. They said that they were very powerful and could

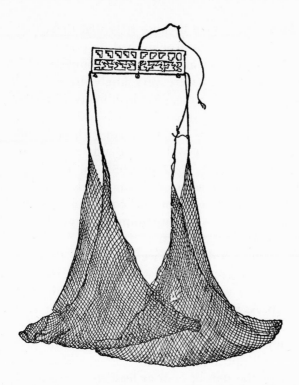

Carved scale with nets. Northern Coast

make the lightning flash from their hands. Now we were quite convinced that they were gods indeed. The merchants offered them gold and clothing and the bearded ones took the gifts, although no lightning flashed from their hands. All the same I could not take my eyes off them, and when the two Indians asked me if I would like to come with them on board the ship, I climbed up the ladder which they threw over the side, as in a dream. When I was on deck the bearded captain of the ship asked me if I wished to stay with them. It seemed to be a better thing to sail with gods than with merchants, and so I remained. Their ship traveled much faster than the raft. Soon my fellow countrymen had disappeared from sight.

The captain of the ship was called Bartolomé Ruiz and before long I learned the names of the other bearded ones. Both the Indians had been given Spanish names, and I too was given one—Felipillo. That was on the Isle of Gallo. There were bearded men there other than those on board the ship, including the field chaplain, Friar Vicente Valverde, who baptized me. But the most important man on that island was their leader, Francisco Pizarro.

Pizarro was a great commander and nothing could deter him from carrying out his plans. On the Isle of Gallo I soon saw that the men did not live like gods. Indeed, their condition was terrible. They were all hungry and many of them were sick. There were quarrels among them, especially between Pizarro and a man who had only one eye and was called Diego de Almagro. He tried to persuade the others to leave Pizarro and go back to Panama. Then Pizarro drew his dagger and marked a line with it in the sand. "Let every man choose for himself. If, like me, you will never give in, step over to my side." There were thirteen who did so, including Ruiz, and they stayed with Pizarro. The others sailed away from the island to Panama from whence they had come with their ship. I was one of those who stayed with Pizarro, although I did not yet count because I did not know enough Spanish. But one thing I had grasped from the very beginning. Pizarro was a man for whom nothing was impossible. He bided his time on that island where there was nothing but rocks and a few trees and water, and where the only living creatures were hares and birds. After a few months, we all looked like ghosts—that is, all except Pizarro. His eyes glowed not with hunger but with fire, with a flame which kept us all alive.

Gradually I began to understand what the fourteen men

were saying. I learned that Pizarro and Almagro had already made one attempt to reach Peru, but that it had come to grief. That was two years before and they had been defeated by the jungle and the swamps, by hunger, rain, and mud. There were many days when the only food was a couple of corncobs per head and they had to eat roots and wild herbs in order to survive. Their days were threatened by poisoned arrows and by snakes, by beasts of prey and vampire bats as well as clouds of mosquitoes.

Of one hundred and fifty men who set out, only fifty had returned to Panama. Pizarro had been wounded seven times and Almagro had lost an eye. That had not prevented them from trying a second time. And now "the fourteen from the Isle of Gallo" were hoping for a ship which would take them south, to the land from which I had come. We had to wait more than twenty weeks for it.

The Spaniards nicknamed me Lenguilla, or "Little Tongue," because I learned their language so quickly. Soon I knew three languages: Spanish, my mother tongue, and the language of the Incas. For once we had been an independent tribe with a language and customs of our own, and it was only when my father was about thirteen that his people had been conquered. From that day on, we had to learn the Inca language and live different lives, and our prince became a vassal, a *curaca*, of the Inca, and had to do what the Inca told him. There was no one more powerful than the Inca, or so we believed, but since I had met the bearded men, I knew differently. They were stronger than the Inca. They were invincible.

The Isle of Gallo had become a hell for them, but they stuck it out, and at last the ship they were waiting for arrived. Now we sailed for my town, Tumbes, and I was no longer a nobody; I was Pizarro's interpreter.

Inca-style coat. Nazca Valley

Mochica jug in the shape of a bearded god

Tumbes lay on the river of the same name among fields and gardens. It was a beautiful city, and far in the distance gleamed the white mountains. The Spaniards cast anchor off shore and gazed across at the town as if it were Paradise. A flotilla of balsa rafts came toward us with golden masks at the mastheads and wide sails spread. I explained to the bearded men that these were the warriors of Tumbes who were setting out on an expedition to wage war against the Isle of Puná. The rafts came close to our ships and I hailed

Suspension bridge. Apurimac region

27

the warriors. I told them that we did not come as enemies but that these white men were the sons of gods. They were so confused that they laid down their weapons and soon we were surrounded by rafts. The Tumbes warriors looked up and saw the white men outlined against the sky. I told the Indians that my masters could make lightning flash from their hands, and Pizarro invited their leaders to come on board. When they saw that Pizarro was a friendly god, they put off their campaign against Puná and returned to the town. Other rafts soon came out bringing the *curaca*'s envoys. They brought us corn and bananas, potatoes, fish, game, and llamas, as well as an invitation from the prince to visit him. The Spaniards had never seen llamas before. One of them gave a llama a push and the animal spat at him.

Next morning, Pizarro allowed a Spaniard and a Negro, who had come with us from Panama, to row across to the town and I went with them. The Spaniard took a pig and the Negro a cock, to present to the *curaca* in return for his gifts. The shore was dark with people. They could hardly contain their wonder. When I assured them that the white man was a kindly god, they touched his beard reverently. But they tried to wash the Negro's face clean and he laughed and flashed his white teeth. Suddenly the cock started beating its wings and crowing. Everyone flocked around and asked me what the bird had said.

Then the Spaniard, the Negro, the pig, the cock, and I went to the *curaca,* accompanied by the vast crowd. Now it was the Spaniard's turn to be astonished. He marveled at the houses which were built like fortresses, at the temple and the great citadel. The guards led us inside the *curaca*'s palace, and when the Spaniard saw the walls gleaming with gold and silver, I saw his eyes sparkle with greed. The *curaca* entertained his guests and gave them presents.

The next day, Pizarro sent an officer on horseback into the town. He wore a suit of armor that blazed like fire in the

28

The conquerors on their way to Peru
(from Poma de Ayala's book)

glory of the sun. "Illa-Ticsi! God of lightning!" cried the crowd when they saw the captain. When I told him what it was they were shouting, he had a plank placed against a wall and fired at it with his gun. The wood was splintered and again the people cried, "The god of lightning!" for they had seen the flash from his hands. The officer took careful note of the city. He observed that the fortress had triple walls built of stone and that many of the blocks were taller than himself. He went inside the temple and saw all the gold. He returned to the ship, satisfied.

On the third day, Pizarro himself entered the town. Wait-

29

ing for him in the *curaca's* palace was an Inca prince. He wore golden disks dangling from his ears, and the lobes were so distended by the weight of the gold that the Spaniards called him *orejón,* which means "big ears."

Pizarro gave the prince a present for the Inca, an iron ax. The *orejón* looked at it in great bewilderment, for he had never seen iron before. The *curaca* gave a feast for the Spaniards and two of them allowed themselves to be persuaded to remain on land. It was agreed that they should stay there until Pizarro returned, for he had every intention of coming back.

On the voyage back to Panama, Pizarro was the guest of a princess who demanded hostages before she would allow the Spaniards to land. She waited on her guest herself, and she was overjoyed when Pizarro ordered trumpets and drums to be sounded and the Spanish flag hoisted, although she had no idea what it meant. When Pizarro declared to her that in future her overlord was no longer the Inca but the King of Spain, I translated: "The white men come from another world and they are your friends." Thus the princess was satisfied and so was Pizarro.

He knew enough now. If there was so much gold in Tumbes, how much more must there be in Cuzco where the Inca had his capital! Pizarro had discovered that the realm of the Incas was far larger than Spain and he was determined to wrest it from the reigning emperor. I could tell that by everything he did. Hardly had he landed in Panama when he set sail again, this time for Spain, and he took me with him. He had sent presents and dispatches ahead of us to the King and this turned out to be a wise move. For as soon as he set foot on Spanish soil he was arrested on account of an old debt.

I saw how they led him away to the debtors' prison, and then I learned many things about him which I had not known before. His father was a common soldier who had

Musicians in festival costume. Mochica painting

risen to be a colonel, but he had never bothered about
Francisco nor his other sons. Francisco had grown up as a
swineherd, but he had become a soldier later. He had con-
tracted debts while he was in the army and had run away to
Panama. Now his creditors had him arrested.

When the King heard about the imprisonment, he had
Pizarro released very quickly and gave him everything he
needed for his expedition: a title, a few ships, and full
authority to conquer the land of the Incas for his king and
for the true God in whom the Spaniards believed. Of all the
gold waiting for the conqueror in Peru, the King demanded
only one-fifth. Pizarro was appointed Governor of Peru, although not a single village there had been captured so far.

Pizarro sailed back to Panama with all possible speed,
taking with him four of his brothers. At the beginning of the
year 1531, he set sail a third time for the south. He landed
on the coast about halfway to Tumbes, where there were no
towns but only jungle villages. The Spaniards invaded these
villages and looted them for emeralds as big as pigeons'

31

eggs, which they struck with iron hammers to see if they were genuine. For six months the jungle held them back and they were as near starvation as on the Isle of Gallo. Pizarro had sent one ship back to Panama laden with booty, but it was many weeks before it returned with provisions on board. It also brought reinforcements led by Hernando de Soto, an officer on whom Pizarro could rely. Now we set off once more for Tumbes, where we arrived on May 13, 1532.

I did not recognize my home town when we got there. Where houses had once stood, there was nothing but crumbling walls. Only the citadel remained undamaged. Warriors from the Isle of Puná had invaded the town and laid it waste. But once more rafts came out of the harbor to meet us and again Pizarro invited the leaders on board and entertained them. They then offered to take the Spaniards ashore, but when the white men were split up into little groups on the various rafts, the Indians drew their weapons. There were dead on both sides, especially among the Indians, for the Spaniards were so embittered at such treachery that they fought like madmen, and they had superior arms.

After a time, the *curaca* who had been driven out by the men from Puná returned to the ruined city. Pizarro learned from him that the two Spaniards who had remained behind in Tumbes had been carried off into the interior by order of the Inca, Atahualpa.

"We shall do everything we can to find them," Pizarro assured him. Then he was silent for a long time, for there was great news to hear. As the *curaca* spoke and I interpreted, Pizarro did not take his eyes off the two of us. This is what had happened.

The old Inca, Huayna Capac, who had conquered the city of Tumbes in my father's time, was dead. He had died in Quito, the kingdom which he had conquered. Before he died, he summoned his son Huáscar and bequeathed to him

32

the greater part of his domain, but not the whole kingdom. Quito and other territories in the north he presented to Atahualpa, another son, whose mother had been a princess in Quito.

"You must know what 'Atahualpa' means," said the *curaca*, "for he has lived up to his name in the last few years. 'Atahualpa' means a fighting cock. At first he remained in Quito while his brother Huáscar reigned in the old Inca capital, Cuzco. But gradually the two brothers came to hate each other so much that each swore he would drink from his brother's skull.

"Before long their armies attacked each other and at first the war went in Huáscar's favor and Atahualpa fell into his hands. But he escaped again, for his wives helped him to turn himself into a snake, so they say, and since then he has been more feared than ever."

It seems that Atahualpa's generals were experienced soldiers who had already conquered much land for his father. And these generals were responsible for defeating Huáscar's army at the Mountain of the Dead near Cuzco. They laid an ambush for Huáscar and he was trapped. Atahualpa, the rebel, made himself Inca and he took a terrible vengeance on Huáscar. He exterminated the whole of his family, and the defeated man was bound to a stake and his eyes propped open, so that he was forced to watch the slaughter. Girls with green branches in their hands came to beg for their fathers' lives, but they found no mercy. Then Huáscar prayed to Viracocha, the bearded god, that he would punish Atahualpa. The *curaca* of Tumbes looked Pizarro straight in the eyes. "And now you have come to bring him to justice," he said.

Pizarro said nothing. So much was going on inside him that his eyes looked blank, but a few minutes later they shone with that same ardor which had gripped "The Thirteen" on the Isle of Gallo. Now that fire carried us with him into the great adventure. On the twenty-fourth of September 1953 he set out with one hundred and sixty-eight men and sixty-three horses to the place where Atahualpa was in residence, Cajamarca, a city in the high mountains where there are hot springs.

The tribes through whose territory we passed had not been subjects of the Inca for long. For them, too, these bearded men were the sons of Viracocha who had come across the seas to punish Atahualpa. Many Indians joined us as we traveled along the roads which led to Cuzco. These roads were paved and bordered by walls against the encroachments of the desert. All along them there were storehouses which contained ample provisions—in fact, everything the Spaniards needed. They were amazed to see what a well-governed country it was, and how thoughtfully the Inca cared for his people, so that even the Spaniards benefitted from his foresight.

After a time, the going grew hard. We had reached the high mountains and the road grew into a giant stairway, which was designed for bearers and llamas but was quite unsuitable for horses. They had to be led by the bridle. The Spaniards were horrified when they saw the abyss which followed the road. There's no going back now, they thought,

Symbols for resthouses and storerooms (from Poma de Ayala's book)

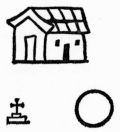

and every one of them realized it, not only Pizarro. And I too, for now I was one of them, one of the band of men out to fight against Atahualpa. My eyes scoured the precipices furtively to see if the Inca's men might not be waiting to attack us from cover, for I knew that the Inca was a mighty ruler. But we were never ambushed, and far from sending an army to stop us, Atahualpa sent ambassadors to meet us. The first carried dainties such as the Inca liked to eat and clothes embroidered with gold. The second carried miniature fortresses made of stone. *These are waiting for you* . . .

Pizarro smiled at the gifts as if they were toys and he was still smiling as he accepted the Inca's invitation to come to Cajamarca. He sent him a little chain as a gift.

On November 15, 1532, we had climbed the mountain road and Cajamarca lay before us, a city with a fortress guarding it. Nothing stirred. The town was deserted. But the heights which dominated it were alive with soldiers. It looked as if the mountainsides were covered with huge snowflakes, for Atahualpa's army had pitched their tents up there, an army of many thousands. Pizarro addressed his one hundred and sixty-eight men. He told them they must pluck fear from their hearts like a weed, leaving room only for the light of truth to flower there and for victory. And so we advanced into Cajamarca, which Atahualpa had evacuated. The houses, streets, and squares were all silent. The Spaniards pried into the houses which were open and empty— like a trap. And behind us, the mountains walled us in. There was no retreat.

There was no one there to bid us welcome, but Pizarro did not waver. He sent me together with Hernando de Soto and a few officers into the Inca's camp while he himself climbed a tower to follow the course of events. It began to rain.

We rode toward the great white snowflakes and as we drew near, thousands of warriors parted to leave a broad avenue open for us. This sinister pathway opened out into a larger square, hemmed in by solid ranks of soldiers as if by a wall. In the middle sat the Inca on his golden stool, surrounded by his courtiers and his wives. Around his forehead he wore the red fringed headband, the *borla,* which was the symbol of his power. Above it sparkled a diadem of gold set with diamonds and rubies and trimmed with feathers. He wore a necklace of emeralds, each one bigger than a finger joint, and on his breast shone a great sun. His robe was woven through with gold. The Inca was set in gold, like a jewel in a ring.

Hernando de Soto delivered Pizarro's message. Atahualpa did not deign to raise his eyes. Then a second troop of Spanish officers arrived with Hernando Pizarro at their head. As soon as the Inca heard that this was Pizarro's brother, he looked up. He also looked at De Soto now and there was no enmity in his glance. He looked for friendship with both Spaniards and he found it. Both remained his friends until death.

The Inca spoke to the two leaders and offered them hospitality. Maidens as beautiful as the sun offered them *chicha* to drink from golden goblets. The Inca admired De Soto's horse, so the Spaniard remounted and the Inca and his assembled army all held their breath as De Soto galloped straight at the Inca. Only at the last moment did he pull up, and so sharply that the horse reared and wisps of foam from its mouth bespattered the sun on the Inca's breast. Later the Inca himself told us that several of his soldiers who had recoiled instinctively had paid with their lives that same day, for their lack of self-control. As we rode away, we had the Inca's word that he would return to Cajamarca next day—with his army.

Night set in. It grew very cold. The hillside which by day had looked as if it were covered with snow was now spread over with blazing red dots burning one beside the other. More campfires burned on the hills behind us. The Inca had enclosed us in a ring of flame. Not one of the one hundred and sixty-eight slept that night.

In the morning, Valverde recited Mass and then Pizarro concealed the bulk of his officers and men in various hiding places all around the square so that escape was impossible for anyone who entered it. The horses had big bells tied to them to make them more terrifying. Pedro de Candia stood ready behind his cannon which had been placed in position near the fortress. Everything was ready for the great battle.

The Inca did not come. The tents and campfires had disappeared from the mountainsides and where they had been we could see the glow of the broad bands of red clay which streaked the soil. We waited as patiently as we could, but the sun was high in the sky before the Inca's army started to move. We saw them advancing for five hours like a sluggish river, and then they came to a halt before Cajamarca. Pizarro challenged the Inca to appear. At that, Atahualpa approached the great square, accompanied by five thousand men. Three hundred Indians swept the roadway before them. Then came singers, groups of dancers, court officials, and finally, surrounded by his bodyguard, Atahualpa himself, borne along

Kero *(goblet) from the Inca period*

in a golden litter with a canopy of costly tapestry sparkling with precious stones. Around him were massed his thousands of soldiers with their spears, maces, swords, and sticks from which hung a cluster of heavy round stones. These were slung at the enemy when the soldiers moved into battle.

Pedro de Candia gazed down at the procession, at the overwhelming superiority of the Indians, and the cavalry stared down from their horses. Some of the Spaniards seemed so agitated that they did not know what they were doing. At a sign from Atahualpa, the dancers stopped and the singers fell silent. It grew so still in the square, it might have been Death himself who had entered.

Then Father Valverde stepped forward, and with him Captain Aldana and I, as Pizarro had arranged. Valverde addressed a sermon to the Inca, in which he said that the God of the Spaniards was the one true God and a Three-in-One God, and that the Spanish King had been placed on this earth to become the Inca's overlord. I translated as best I could, but it was difficult for me to understand myself what the chaplain meant by the Holy Trinity.

The Inca shook his head. Thereupon Valverde handed to him the book which is called the Bible. The Inca held it to his ear. "It does not speak to me," he replied and let it fall. Then he began to protest against the Spaniards' conduct. The Spaniards had come by force, he said, and looted many houses. Aldana told the Inca not to waste time in idle complaints but to hand over his realm to the Spanish King. Then Atahualpa demanded to see Aldana's sword. The captain drew it and held it out to the Inca with the naked blade uppermost. Atahualpa grasped the sharp steel and pushed the sword aside. His hand started bleeding. At this, Pizarro gave a great cry: "Santiago and at them!" Pedro de Candia fired his cannon; the soldiers broke out of hiding. The Inca and his troops stood there dumbfounded, as if Pizarro's battlecry had turned them to stone. For the second time,

Pizarro appeared to me like a god, a being who could achieve anything. The Inca lost his voice. His litter bearers were cut down like cattle. One Spaniard raised his dagger to strike the Inca, but Pizarro himself threw up his arm and caught the blow. This was the only wound which any Spaniard received that day. In half an hour every soldier who had accompanied Atahualpa was dead and the Inca was taken prisoner, like his brother Huáscar, from whom he had seized power. Now it was his turn to fall into a conqueror's hands.

Valverde reading the Bible to Atahualpa. On the right is Felipillo (from Poma de Ayala's book)

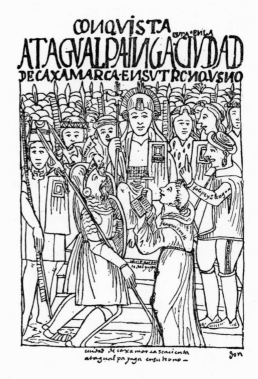

The great square was red with blood, and in the light of the setting sun the houses of Cajamarca and the mountainsides gleamed with crimson. Pizarro conducted the Inca to the finest palace in Cajamarca, the Snake Palace. There the royal prisoner was installed with his wives, his precious household goods, and his sumptuous clothing. Spanish sentries kept guard all around the royal residence. This time, there was no likelihood of turning into a snake!

That evening, Atahualpa dined with Pizarro exactly as it had been arranged. And in the days that followed, Pizarro treated the Inca like a prince. He taught him how to play chess, and the words of the catechism, and Pizarro often spoke of his God. Atahualpa could see by now that the Spanish God was much stronger than Viracocha or any of the other gods they still worshipped in Peru at that time. Atahualpa was furious with them all, and particularly with Pachacamac, who he said had deceived him. "That liar" was what he called him, for his oracle had prophesied that no one would ever vanquish the Inca Atahualpa.

Valverde also talked to the Inca about the Spanish God, but Atahualpa soon saw that the conquerors revered another god too. They worshipped gold. So he made a proposal to Pizarro. He offered to fill the great room in which he dwelt to a height of nine feet with gold and the two adjoining rooms with silver as a ransom in exchange for his freedom. The Inca himself marked the line along the walls and Pizarro's notary drew up a contract putting everything in writing. The Inca asked for two months' grace.

Rivers of gold and silver began to flow toward Cajamarca. Bearers and llama caravans streamed from every point of the compass, but especially from Cuzco. The nobles carried their contributions personally. They appeared barefoot before Atahualpa and flung themselves at his feet as if he were still their sovereign lord and not a captive bound by invisible chains. Among the treasure were golden vessels weighing sixty pounds apiece. The Inca's face brightened in the gleam of so much gold.

One day, Pizarro confronted the Inca with a question. "Where is your brother Huáscar?" he asked. The Inca lied. "He is no longer alive," he replied, and as Pizarro believed him, Atahualpa quickly sent a message to Jauja where Huáscar was still a prisoner, with the orders that he should be done away with. So Huáscar was drowned in the River Yanamayo and disappeared without a trace. But somehow or other the facts were reported back to Pizarro.

The deception did not save Atahualpa, nor indeed did all the gold he offered to the conquerors. It was a colossal ransom, over a million pesos in gold and almost fifty thousand marks in silver, apart from the Inca's throne, whose value could hardly be assessed.

When the ransom was assembled, the Inca asked for his freedom and Hernando Pizarro, Hernando de Soto, and nine others pleaded for him. They were packed off to various parts of the country in a great hurry, with orders to quell various uprisings, for there was widespread rebellion against the invaders. By the time they returned, Atahualpa was dead. In vain had he tried to impress his captors. "Do you believe that a single hand will be lifted for you unless I will it?" he insisted. "In my kingdom, not a bird flies, not a leaf stirs, but at my command!" It was of no avail. Atahualpa was a lost man. The Spaniards were afraid that once the Inca was freed, he would take away from them everything he had given them as a helpless prisoner. They were afraid, too, for their own lives. After all, had not Atahualpa done away with his own brother with great cruelty? So they found the last of the Incas guilty of various crimes and condemned him to death. The only favor granted was to allow him to choose if he would prefer to be burned at the stake, or, if he would consent to be baptized, to die by the garotte.

So Atahualpa allowed himself to be baptized, for then he

would not disappear physically from this world. Like all his ancestors, he would still reign on as a mummy with a golden mask over his face. Pizarro himself stood as godfather at the christening and he gave the Inca his own name as a gift. The ceremony over, Francisco Pizarro stood by Francisco Atahualpa while the Inca was strangled to death, and all the Spaniards gathered around the grave, dressed in deep mourning.

Next morning, the corpse had disappeared. Faithful subjects had carried it away and no Spaniard ever found it. Atahualpa's wives followed him to their graves, and from that day on, he ruled from a throne which was known only to his own people.

Why did Pizarro have the Inca executed when he had him safe in his hands? I, Felipillo, know of one of the reasons. Once Pizarro had been shown up in front of the Inca and I was present. The Inca had asked a sentry if all Spaniards could read and write. In reply, the soldier had written the name of God on his thumbnail and one after the other, all those who passed had read the word on the sentry's nail— all except one who could not read and whose name was Francisco Pizarro. He had never forgiven Atahualpa after that.

When Atahualpa was dead, Pizarro campaigned on until the heart of the kingdom lay before him. On November 15, 1533, exactly one year after the entry into Cajamarca, and nine years after the first attempt to enter the unknown kingdom of Peru, the conquerors entered the capital city of Cuzco. No one barred their way, no one stopped them from looting the Inca's palace and the temples. Goblets, ewers, golden dishes ornamented with birds, lizards, and lobsters, "as if they were alive in the sea," golden llamas, golden statues of women "as beautiful as if they were real," all the

Tambomachay, an Inca residence near Cuzco. "The Inca's Bath"

Stone jar in the shape of a llama, stylized. Inca period

golden friezes from the temples: everything fell as booty
to the conquerors. From the chief temple of the kingdom,
the House of Gold, they tore down seven hundred platters
of pure gold, images of the sun, the moon, and the stars and
of thunder and lightning, and the golden thrones which
stood there for the Inca mummies.

Around the golden temple there was a hanging garden,
and these terraces were the greatest of all the golden marvels
of Peru. In this garden there were flowers, bushes and trees,
corn and tobacco plants, stones and grass, hares, birds,
lizards and snakes, llamas and herdsmen, and fountains—all
made out of solid gold. It was a golden garden for the Inca

*(Above) Part of the stonework of the triple walls which guarded
Sacsahuamán*
*(Below) "The Inca's Throne," an ancient shrine near Sacsa-
huamán*

43

and the Sun. Not a single corncob has survived. The golden birds and lizards all vanished from the walls of the palace. Cuzco was no longer the golden heart of the kingdom of the Incas.

The goldsmiths in Cajamarca had needed a whole month to melt down the Inca's ransom into bullion. Every Spanish officer had received 8,880 gold pesos as his share and the common soldiers half that amount. In Cuzco, the plunder was even greater. The Spaniards gorged themselves with gold, but it left them hungrier than ever. They removed the golden palings which had marked the empire's frontiers and kept evil spirits away from the realm. As they had no iron to shoe their horses, they used silver instead. But in spite of the vast treasure that came their way, I know full well that much gold escaped their hands. There were loads of gold on the way to Cajamarca when Atahualpa's death became known, and these were never found by the Spaniards. Nor were the three hundred consignments hidden below the snowy peak of Pachatusan. They found no trace of the golden chain which Huayna Capac had had forged at Huáscar's birth and which needed ten men to carry it. It lay at the bottom of a mountain lake which has never betrayed its secret.

The gold which fell into the hands of the *conquistadores* brought them little happiness. For each in turn, the hour struck when he cursed gold as "the filth of the gods, which is death to those who touch it." The eleven who had pleaded for the Inca were all murdered before long. So was the chaplain, Valverde, who had baptized Atahualpa. The Indians who caught him poured molten gold into his eyes. Almagro was beheaded on Pizarro's orders, and supporters of Almagro stabbed Pizarro to death in revenge. My turn came then, for I was killed by the same mob. They did not know that they were carrying out Atahualpa's wishes, for he had demanded my death from Pizarro when one of his wives gave me an encouraging look and so provoked Atahualpa's hatred.

The last of the Incas thought that I was a traitor and he was right. Too late, I came to see that these bearded men were no gods but wolves, who would spring at each other's throats or murder a comrade for a handful of gold. What did they care if gold was sacred to the Inca people! In their lust for it, they tore down the very image of the god who had made the stars and the world of men.

I came with the Spaniards and I stayed with them to the end. But now I know that they were not sent by Viracocha. They came to destroy the Kingdom of the Sun, which the Sons of the Sun had built.

The Sons of the Sun

A few decades after the conquest of Peru, a certain Spaniard made an exceptionally lucky find. His name was Polo de Ondegardo and he had been appointed as a judge in Cuzco. The Viceroy of Peru laid upon him the special task of finding out how the Indians had lived while the Sons of the Sun were in power, and Ondegardo interrogated many Indians, including the descendants of the Inca's family. In his search for people who could give him information, Ondegardo entered many houses and former palaces. In the district of Tococache, there was one large building where, in the days of the Incas, girls had been educated for service in the temples. And there, hidden away, Ondegardo discovered five mummies wrapped in costly shrouds. Three of them had golden masks and wore the royal headband, the red *borla,* around their foreheads. There were other signs, too, that made it clear that Ondegardo had discovered the mummies of three Incas.

A crowd gathered in the big square outside the house and

members of the Inca nobility told the judge that these were the mummies of Viracocha Inca, Tupac Yupanqui, and Huayna Capac and of two of their queens. The people stood around in deep silence and did not dare to raise their eyes to look at the Sons of the Sun.

The golden masks were soon melted down. The conquerors exercised their rights as victors and many were convinced that they had come as liberators, to set free the people whom the Incas had oppressed. Few Spaniards admitted that they had come as destroyers, too. Pedro Pizarro, a cousin of Francisco, who saw the last Inca day after day, and who met many Inca princes in Cuzco, declared that there were no better rulers on earth than the Incas, none who had the welfare of their people more at heart. They were the Sons of the Sun God and his regents.

In the years that followed, many Spaniards, like Ondegardo, traveled up and down Peru and wrote about what they had discovered. Priests and officials, administrators, soldiers, and sailors all wrote chronicles in which they recorded what they had seen and been told of in the land of the Incas.

The most astute of all these writers was Pedro de Cieza de León. He ran away from Spain when he was fifteen years old and eventually reached Peru. He became an officer, fought in Colombia, and under the leadership of the only Spaniard who took no gold for himself, the ambassador Gasca, he fought to suppress those *conquistadores* who were rebelling against the King of Spain. "Often I used to plague myself with writing while the others slept," Cieza tells us. "Neither sickness nor exhaustion, neither the rough country nor the pangs of hunger, could stop me from following the banner of Spain and from writing."

And not only Spaniards wrote books. There were chroniclers who had noble Inca blood in their veins. Garcilaso de la Vega was born a few years after the Spaniards had entered the country, the son of a Spanish colonel and a granddaugh-

47

ter of Huayna Capac. His father kept open house equally for Spaniards and for the Inca aristocracy. When he was twenty, Garcilaso was sent to Spain, where he was nicknamed "The Inca." In his old age, he wrote a book in which he described the eleven rulers who had held the rank of Inca before Huáscar and Atahualpa, the true Sons of the Sun. Poma de Ayala, another descendant of the Incas, also wrote a book, and in it he tried to portray his ancestors in as favorable a light as possible.

The Sons of the Sun ruled for three centuries, and they needed the best part of the first two hundred years to consolidate their footing among the other mountain tribes. So it was in less than one hundred years that Pachacuti, Tupac Yupanqui, and Huayna Capac, the "world-changers," created by their conquest an empire almost four times the size of Spain.

But how did it start? What was the origin of this race, the Quechua people, who succeeded in conquering tribe after tribe? Where did the Incas come from?

The Indian mythology has two versions. In one they emerged from a cave. In another, they climbed from the middle one of three windows. The legend goes like this. In the olden days, when the human race still lived like packs of wild animals, four men and four women, who called each other brothers and sisters, climbed through that window. The brothers were named Manco Capac, Auca, Cachi, and Uchu. The eldest sister was called Mama Ocllo by the others. From the two side windows came the Indian tribes of Maras and Tambo, and before their eyes a miracle occurred. The Sun God came down to earth, clothed Manco Capac in golden armor, and handed him a golden staff. "You and your brothers are my sons," he said. "Go out into the world and subdue all the tribes." Then he gave them kernels of corn. "Find a land where corn will flourish," he went on, "and there you must build a city for yourselves and a temple for

48

me, your father." The Sun God gave the four brothers golden disks to wear as ear pendants. Then he stepped down from the rock on which he stood and returned to his golden house, the sun.

Manco Capac and his brothers and sisters now set out to find the fertile land. The place where they had been born and were summoned to rule the world by the Sun God, they called Paccari-Tampu, "the place of our origin." Manco took Ocllo to wife and for a long time they wandered on. When they reached the mountain height of Huanacauri, a quarrel started. Manco, Auca, and Uchu united against Cachi, whom

Manco Capac, the first Inca (from Poma de Ayala's book)

they feared because he was a magician. They enticed him into a cave and then blocked up the entrance with heavy boulders. Cachi was so enraged that he turned himself into stone. The youngest brother, Uchu, remained on Huanacauri, and there he served the sun until he, too, was turned to stone. The same fate overtook Auca before they reached their destination. Only Manco Capac and Mama Ocllo remained. She took the golden staff and hurled it, and it fell in the Valley of Cuzco. There it buried itself so deeply in the ground that they could find no trace of it, and so they took it as an omen that they should settle in Cuzco.

Manco Capac laid out fields and built dams to curb the wild waters which came pouring down from the glaciers. He subdued the wild tribes who lived in the region and taught them what he had learned from his mother, for she could understand the language of the trees, the lakes, and even the rocks, and she had asked the seeds what plants lay within them. And Manco Capac taught the people how to live as human beings, as men.

As the Sun God had charged him, he founded a city in the midst of the fertile earth, Cuzco, the fourfold, "the town of the four directions." The higher part of the town was known as Hurin and the lower sectors were called Hanan. In Hanan he built a beautiful house for the Sun God, and when his hour came, Manco too was turned to stone.

Manco's descendants ruled as befitted the Children of the Sun and tried to extend their territory. As they were not yet strong enough to rely on a policy of armed aggression, they followed the behest of the Sun God, not to vanquish other tribes but to teach them how men should live. So they made alliances and married the daughters of neighboring chieftains of other clans, and so enlarged their territory without the use of force.

Only the fourth and fifth Incas felt secure enough to send

their armies far beyond Cuzco, especially to the south where the Collas lived. The Inca soldiers crossed Lake Titicaca in their boats of reeds. They climbed icy peaks and they lived on grass. By night, they saw the glow of furnaces, for the Collas were skilled smiths and knew how to work in gold and silver, in copper and lead. They found a way of smelting silver by the use of lead, which they called *curuchec,* or "that which makes to flow." The Incas built fortresses in Colla country, for soon it was Inca territory and the Collas had to live as the Incas wished.

The Incas called their own language *runa simi,* or "the human tongue." All those who became their subjects had to learn this language and everyone was equal before the Inca. In this way, the Inca people was welded out of many different tribes.

When the sixth Inca, Inca Roca, came to power, his warriors pushed forward into the lands of the torrid zones, the jungle. They had slung a huge suspension bridge across the Apurimac River and the Inca power had grown so great that many tribes came over to them without fighting. They bowed low as soon as the Sons of the Sun entered their land, for the Inca came like a god, bearing the morning star in his hand.

Inca Roca pushed on as far as the coast, and from there he brought back two things which became very important in the lives of his people. They were coca and guano. Coca is a powerful and stimulating shrub which holds hunger at bay, and guano is bird manure which makes the seed much more fertile even in the highlands. The sixth Inca built his palace in the middle of Hurin, the upper section of the capital; it was constructed of huge blocks of stone, one of which can still be seen, the famous twelve-cornered stone of Cuzco. Until then, the Incas had lived in Hanan and the priests too. Now the Inca moved one step higher and he called the kingdom Tawantinsuyu, "Land of the Four Directions." By this, the Inca meant that his kingdom embraced the four quarters of the earth—in fact, the whole world.

But they had not got quite so far yet. There were still states on their borders who did not wish to become the Inca's subjects. That was made clear in the reign of the seventh Inca, Yahuar Huacac, "the one who weeps tears of blood." The Inca had been given this nickname as a child. A mortal enemy of his father's had abducted him and one day, in the mountain eyrie where he was kept a prisoner, the boy had wept tears of blood. This had made such an impression on his captor that he released the child, for the sight of tears had reminded the kidnapper of the god of all creation, who has traces of tears beneath his eyes, a sign that all life springs from him.

Yahuar Huacac was a peace-loving ruler who did not think in terms of war and conquest. When a plague devastated the country, he traveled through the land, comforting his people. When enemies attacked, he drove them back to the frontiers, but he did not crush them into subjection. This Inca, however, had a son who was quite the opposite in character. When the boy was only twelve years old, he fought with grown men and he even overturned the images of the gods. To punish him, his father sent him up into the *puna,* the desolate grasslands high in the mountains, and there the youth had to tend his father's llamas. In the wilderness, the young prince communed with himself. One evening he fell asleep beneath a canopy of overhanging rock, and just as the sun was rising next day the prince was suddenly awakened. He looked up in surprise and from the rock face there emerged a pale countenance with bright eyes and a beard. It was Viracocha, the bearded god. "Go back to Cuzco," the god told the prince. "Tell your father that the Chancas are coming to destroy his kingdom." Then the god faded back into the rock and the prince went to his father and warned him. But the Inca sent his son back to his herds. He did not believe what the lad had told him.

The Chancas came. They came sweeping through the land with such overwhelming might that the weeper of blood had to surrender his capital in order to save his life.

The prince came down from the *puna* a second time, but this time he collected an army and marched against the Chancas. There was a pitched battle and other tribes watched from a distance, waiting to see who would be victorious, so that they could rally to the winning side. The prince had placed a reserve of troops concealed in an ambush, and with the rest of his force he attacked the Chancas in the name of Viracocha. The battle remained indecisive until noon. Then, as the sun blazed forth and dazzled the Chanca army, the Inca prince pressed so deep inside the enemy's lines that he was able to lay hands on their god, a jaguar made of wood. The warriors defending it had monsters painted on their shields, but as the Inca prince seized their god and the deity did nothing to punish such sacrilege, the Chancas turned and fled. Now the reserves broke out of cover and pursued the fleeing enemy, and all the tribes who had been watching joined the victorious army of the Incas. The prince was now powerful enough to take the scarlet fillet from his father's forehead and to place himself on the Inca throne. He called himself Viracocha from now on, in honor of the god to whom he owed his accession. With his own hands he made a golden image of the god, and he had a great temple built for him.

Viracocha Inca was followed by Pachacuti, the man with lion's eyes. Pachacuti means "one who changes the world," and if ever an Inca deserved his name, it was this ninth Inca. He too seized by force the throne which had been intended for his brother, but Pachacuti felt that he had been summoned to rule by the Sun God himself. He warned the Chanca princes: "Keep your hands off Cuzco, for this town belongs to the god without whom nothing on earth lives; without whom you cannot live either."

Pachacuti extended the kingdom far and wide. His tactics were always the same. First of all he sent out spies, then negotiators, and finally his army. Only if the tribe refused to surrender without bloodshed did he prepare for war. Before each campaign started, he fasted for a long time and prayed devoutly. There was never any doubt about the result, for Pachacuti's army was supreme. The subject peoples were forced to supply fighting men for the next conquest and the storehouses were kept stocked with weapons as well as foodstuffs, so that the Inca's army was ready to march at any hour. The farmer simply put down his hoe and his digging stick; put on his helmet, which was made of wood or straw; picked up his shield, which was covered with tapir skin or deerskin; and took sling, spear, and club and set off with his hundred. Inca armies penetrated as far as the source of the Amazon; they invaded the land of the Yuncas, whose towns were situated along the coast; and they entered the "cold province,"

Decoration from an Inca vessel

the land around Cajamarca. Clay models of the conquered territories were prepared, so that the Inca had a relief map of his new acquisitions; and tribes from the mountains, the coastal plains, and the jungle all became his subjects.

One of the coastal gods whom the Incas conquered was Pachacamac, the weather keeper, who was also known as Rimac, the Great Speaker. Pachacuti adopted this deity so that he became an oracle for all the Inca people. But then the emperor built a new house for the Sun God which stood higher than Pachacamac's shrine close by, so that the Inca god dominated the Great Speaker, just as the Inca had supremacy over all other rulers.

The Inca's will was law. Anyone who disobeyed, even if he were the brother of the Inca, like Yupanqui, was punished with death.

Yupanqui was not only the Inca's brother but one of his generals. When the Chancas had been defeated some of them were made to join the Inca's army, and Yupanqui was given command of their troops. It so happened that this fighting force was able to take by storm a particularly obstinate fortress which Inca warriors had failed to capture. The Inca feared that his former enemies would be so flushed with success that they would rise against him. So he gave orders that the successful Chancas were to be surrounded secretly that night and massacred. Yupanqui betrayed this bloody order to the sister of the Chanca leader, and when it was dark, the eight thousand who were to be murdered so treacherously overpowered the guards and escaped. They looted storehouses as they went, and then made their escape into impassable territory. Yupanqui set out to pursue them. Although he conquered several new valleys for the Inca and came back to Cuzco laden with fabulous booty, he was summarily executed and no one protested against such ruthlessness.

Yet the ninth Inca knew how to rule mercifully too. Once on a campaign to the southern coast, a girl took his fancy, but she was about to be married and refused him her favors. The village feared dire punishment, but instead Pachacuti invited the girl to make a wish. She begged for water for the village; Pachacuti had his soldiers lay down their arms there and then and dig canals for irrigation.

Pachacuti had roads and aqueducts built throughout the land; the fields were terraced and great stairways were hewn in the mountainsides to give access to the heights. If the Inca thought that certain areas were underpopulated, he imported colonists, resettling whole tribes where necessary. Through such transfers, which were known as *mitimaes,* the conquered areas were integrated into the kingdom. Cuzco, too, was replanned according to Pachacuti's wishes. He built new temples, observatories, and granaries. He transformed the capital into the golden wonder which made the *conquistadores* gasp with amazement when they saw it. For as the empire grew, bearers and llama caravans brought tribute from more distant gold fields. Pachacuti also enlarged the schools where the sons of the aristocracy were educated and made the qualifying examinations stiffer. Throughout the land the "human tongue" was introduced. Citadels were erected and the old ones refortified with new walls, and secured block by block with bronze cramps. Thus the Inca armored his country against attack so that the people could go about their work with an easy mind. Everything was taken care of, every disaster anticipated, and provision made for wars and earthquakes, for drought and flood. And no one went hungry in Pachacuti's kingdom.

This Inca reigned for thirty-three years, and in those three decades he altered his world completely. He had the events of his reign portrayed on wooden tablets and in tapestry. When he felt his end was near, he placed his son Tupac Yupanqui on the throne. Then he gave orders that he himself was to be carried to a wall of rock near Cuzco where there were three caves. He had the entrance to the middle one set in gold, as a memorial to that cave from which the race of the Incas had once sprung. There he sat down and spoke for the last time with his sons and his grandsons. Envy, he told them, was a fatal sickness, and impatience was a fire which raged in clouded minds, but misfortune was the anvil on which courage was forged. Then, in a soft voice, he sang his own elegy: "Like the lilies of the field, I came to die. A great light shone all around me as long as I blossomed, but now I fade and must go away."

So died the greatest of all the Sons of the Sun. He was buried close to Cuzco in the cave beneath the sacred rock of Kenko, which has the shape of a mountain lion. When the Spaniards approached it, the priests had the tomb walled up and the rock covered over. One thing is certain. If the Spaniards had attempted the conquest of Peru while Pachacuti was emperor, the invaders would have been wiped out and not a trace of them left.

Tupac Yupanqui, the tenth Inca, continued to add new territory to the kingdom, and only one region, the Chimu country, defended itself for long. The Chimu was the mightiest of the kingdoms of the coast, a state with cities, fortresses, and roads. A great wall stretched from the coast up into the mountains, giving the land complete protection from invasion. The Inca was greatly troubled, for he could not see any way of breaching this wall. He conferred with his teachers, the *amautas,* and then he saw the light. "Are not the valleys of the Chimu fed by water from the mountains?" he asked himself. "Without it, would not the whole kingdom become a desert?" So he sent out great numbers of workmen, accompanied by an army of four thousand soldiers. The canals were diverted and the water dried up. Then the Inca sent ambassadors to the Great Chimu and this is what they said in his name: "I, the Son of the Sun, whom all the waters obey, will only allow your rivers to flow again if you will accept my sovereignty."

The Inca and the coya *worshipping the "Three Windows" (from Poma de Ayala's book)*

And so the northern coast fell to the tenth Inca. He might well have rested content with such an acquisition, but in Tumbes he heard that there were lands beyond the western horizon, across the great sea. The Inca consulted the *amautas* and they told him that it was an incredible distance to these lands. But the Inca was eager to put his fortune to the test, to see if his star still shone for him over the sea as it did on land. He fasted for forty days, and he had a fleet of rafts

Indians at Cuzco

built. With them he set out for the west. Those who stayed behind watched anxiously as the rafts disappeared from sight. After six months, one of the Inca's generals, who feared unrest in the land, announced that he had had good news from the fleet. But he was punished for his lie when the Inca finally returned after more than a year's absence. He brought back with him trophies which were considered so important that even when the Spaniards arrived, a sentry of royal blood stood guard over them. Among them was a chair of brass, a horse's skull, and much else that told of lands far beyond Peru, or so the story went.

The tenth Inca acquired many lands without bloodshed, for they yielded to the magic of his name. The eleventh Inca, Huayna Capac, also extended his frontiers without a blow. In less than one hundred years, through three Sons of the Sun, the Inca domain grew to be the greatest kingdom of the New World and six million subjects obeyed Huayna Capac as if he were a god.

In his last years, reports kept coming to the Inca about the bearded men who had come from across the sea. Then from the coast of Peru itself came news of the white men who carried lightning with them. Once the Inca was convinced that the news was true, he was chilled with horror. He locked himself in his room and did not come out until nightfall. The couriers from the coast had said that the bearded men had forced their way into the temples and ransacked them. Nothing, they said, had frightened them away, not even the mountain lions in the cages. The Inca insisted on hearing the report a second time and the messenger told him: "The bearded men stepped into the cages without fear and the mountain lions fawned on them and did not harm them." Then the Inca stood up and tore his mantle. "Out of my sight!" he cried. "Why do you bring such mischief into my

(Above) Llamas
(Below) Indian woman with her children

59

house?" But immediately afterward, he called the runners back again so that they could recite the story for the third time. The Inca did not know what to expect from these invaders. Were they really the sons of Viracocha or were they bringers of evil? Only one thing was sure: no one was strong enough to drive them away.

Then the Inca did something which sealed the destruction of his empire. In arranging for his succession, he did not bequeath the whole country to Huáscar, but set aside the northern provinces for Atahualpa. This laid the foundations for that rivalry which ultimately destroyed both his sons. Huayna Capac died of a plague which had devastated the army campaigning with him in the north. He was the last Inca to be laid to rest with ceremonial rites and carried back to Cuzco as a mummy with a golden countenance.

The Inca was the apex of a perfect pyramid in which every citizen had his precise place. The base consisted of the able-bodied workers, the *purics*, the millions who were virtually indistinguishable, the masses. Over every hundred *purics* there was an overseer, the *camayoc*, who had to see that the Inca's commands were carried out to the letter. For every thousand there was another official and a higher one still for each ten thousand. Above the ten lords of each ten thousand there was a *tucui-ru-cuc*, "one who sees everything." The highest rank of all was that of the *capac apu*. There were four of them, each one the ruler of one of the "quarters of the earth" which composed the Tawantinsuyu, the world of the Incas.

High above them all reigned the Inca, and he alone decided what must be done to please the Sun God. It was as unthinkable that the Inca could err as that the sun could swerve from its course, or so his people believed. Even when the kingdom was split by the fratricidal struggle of Huáscar and his brother, even when Atahualpa had proved how helpless he was to escape from the Spaniards, thousands of his

Huayna Capac, the eleventh Inca (from Poma de Ayala's book)

subjects allowed themselves to be killed for his sake, because he was the Son of the Sun.

No Spaniard ever saw the Inca kingdom in its full glory, but we know what it looked like in the days of the "world-changers" from the writings of the Spanish and Indian chroniclers. Many of these records were lost for centuries. It was as late as 1905 that a German scholar named Pietschmann discovered the chronicle of the sea captain Pedro Sarmiento de Gamboa in a library at Göttingen, and a few years later, he discovered the thick, thousand-page volume of the Inca's

61

grandson, Poma de Ayala, in the Royal Library at Copenhagen. This book is illustrated by hundreds of pictures, and it is from this source more than almost any other that the world of the Incas looks across to ours in the twentieth century.

Pictures from
the world of the Incas

PICTURE ONE: My name is Felipe Huamán Poma de Ayala and I am the young man in the middle of the picture, the one wearing a Spanish cape, Spanish trousers, and a Spanish hat. Like my name, I am half Indian, half Spanish. My mother was the granddaughter of the tenth Inca, the ruler who challenged his star and undertook a great voyage by raft, sailing away into the unknown. My father was a Spaniard, Martín de Ayala. He dressed me in Spanish clothes and sent me to a Spanish school. But he had great sympathy with everything Indian, and when he saw that many Spaniards treated the natives like cattle, he urged me to write this book. He advised me to talk to as many Indians as possible and to learn from them how the people of Peru lived under the Incas. And that is what I have done.

You can see how many people there are pressing around me. Some of them are Inca princes in their rich cloaks, with golden disks in their ears. They clamor around me and lift their hands, saying, "This is what it was like in the old days," and "This is what is happening now. The King of Spain must be told that the Spaniards here are destroying us."

I listened to them and to my mother as well, and then I wrote this book. My father sent it to the King of Spain on May 15, 1587. I do not know if ever King Philip received it personally, for nothing much has changed for the people during my lifetime. Perhaps it was too much effort for the King to read what I wrote, for I must admit that my Spanish is not perfect, and if I could not think of the right word in Spanish I used the Inca term instead. Perhaps what I wrote was difficult to read, but surely the pictures I drew speak for themselves!

PICTURE TWO: Here is the world of the little man, the common laborer on one of his good days. The able-bodied worker was called a *puric,* and I have drawn one carrying the harvest into his house. His son, his wife, and his llamas are helping him. He was not allowed to own more than his hut, a plot of land to keep him from starvation, a pair of llamas and their calf, and perhaps a dog and a few hens as well. I suppose someone will contradict me here and say that hens were only introduced into Peru during my lifetime. But I have made searching inquiries and I know that hens were not uncommon even before the Spanish Conquest. They were used as barter in trade with other countries which the Spaniards had conquered some decades before.

However, it is true that hens were not very important for the workers. The llamas counted for much more, for they are docile creatures and carry their loads without protest; they seek their own food and can go for weeks without water. They can withstand the icy cold at night and they can find a path for themselves anywhere, even along the edge of a glacier. So the *puric* lived on his plot of land with his wife and their pair of llamas. If a son was born, another portion of land was added to his holding, and if a daughter, half that amount. A *puric* could never become rich, but none of them died of hunger. If, in spite of hard work, a *puric* family had not enough to eat, the *camayoc* who was in charge of the allocation of the fields was called to account, for he had failed to carry out the will of the Inca. For the Inca took care of his people. He saw that a house was built for each family, to shelter them from the snow, the wind, and the rain. The very first Inca, Manco Capac, taught his subjects what tasks were to be carried out month by month, and since those days, everyone knew when it was time to till the soil and when to spin wool, when to take the llamas out to pasture, when to harvest corn and potatoes, clean out the wells, and thatch the roof, and when to honor the dead.

65

TRAVAXA
ZARA PAPA APAICVIAIMO
ray julio chacra comacujquilla

In order that work should not be too much of a burden, the Inca ordained three feast days in each month in which everyone could get drunk, and three market days in addition, so that the rural population could come into the town to hear what the Inca had decreed for the period ahead. The Inca distributed salt to the people so that they should enjoy their food, and some was set aside for the llamas, who relished it as well.

I have not forgotten to include the sun in my picture, without which neither the worker nor his field could thrive, nor have I left out the mountains which have produced the Inca people. In a world of rock, the *puric* became hardened, tough, insensitive to cold and to hunger, a highlander with a

66

powerful chest and sturdy bones, and more blood in his veins than they had who lived on the flat coastal strip.

PICTURE THREE: This is the worker on his land, drilling holes in the soil with a pointed digging stick while his wife plants the grains of corn in them. According to an old custom, a woman must do the sowing or nothing will thrive. It was rare for the common man to have two wives, although it was very different for the aristocracy.

Not only was the *puric* wife a farmer like her husband, but it was she who had to carry loads like a beast of burden and to do many other things besides. She had to cook, sew, wash, spin, weave, and grind corn between stones. When it

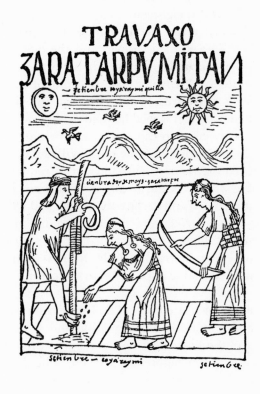

was time to brew *chicha,* or corn beer, she chewed up the kernels of corn and then spat them into a big jar. The saliva helped to make the beer ferment. Of course, it was also the woman's duty to keep the hut clean and to bring up her children. Often children were born on the march, for the women were frequently used as bearers, as I have said. After the birth, the woman would bathe her body in a mountain stream and then wash the baby, having first warmed the icy water in her mouth. That was the only tenderness which she was allowed to show. On the fourth day, the newborn infant was placed in a cradle and carried on its mother's back. It was weaned when it was two, and at fourteen it was given the names which it would carry for the rest of its life. The boys followed their fathers' trade and the girls were given a husband at eighteen.

What was a wedding like? The girl had to place her left foot in a woolen slipper, and the eldest member of the clan lit a fire under a pot. Then he pronounced the following sentence: "It is not good that one of you should freeze while the other burns." And with that, the girl was the wife of the man who had wooed her and made bridal gifts to her father.

Anyone who did not marry voluntarily was compelled to do so. An official came to the village, the *camayoc* perhaps, or even the *tucui-ru-cuc,* and not infrequently the Inca himself. He would beckon to any man and girl from the ranks of the unmarried and declare them man and wife.

The *purics* were not allowed to build houses for themselves. These were provided by the state. But it was the duty of every married couple to have children, for the Inca needed a large population to serve him.

PICTURE FOUR: The boy scaring away birds with a sling and a stone is between nine and twelve years old. At that age, the *puric* boys had to see that the birds did not steal too much corn before the harvest. This boy is wearing a wolf-

68

skin over his head and shoulders. With his whip and his sling he went out into the fields which belonged either to the Sun God, to the Inca, or to the boy's clan, the *ayllu*. Here he learned in play how to kill with a stone from a sling. The boy is proud that he has killed a bird and holds it in his hand.

From twelve to eighteen, the *puric* boys tended the llamas or helped their fathers at work. After eighteen, every *puric* was liable for service when ordered. He had to help with building roads, bridges, canals, and fortresses, and with terracing the mountainsides into agricultural land.

If the Inca decided to transfer a family to another place, the whole household was removed—wife, children, llamas, and all. Often whole villages were transplanted so the "hu-

man tongue" would be spoken there, and so that day by day the vanquished tribe would have under their eyes the example of reliable Inca subjects.

The worker was considered to be able-bodied and fit for any work until he was fifty. After that, he was not expected to do any heavy work, and when over sixty, he was classified as a *punucrucu,* a "frail sleeper," whose only task was to keep an eye on the little children, the ducks, and the guinea pigs. The old people were the responsibility of the whole clan, just like the sick and the insane, and they all had their share in the clan's communal property. The *ayllu* or clan comprised all those to whom the same *huaca* was sacred.

The communal land was marked out with llama bones, and the Inca watched over the whole community so that no *puric* suffered want or violence or was treated unjustly. Where water was scarce, the Inca had it supplied. If the soil was thin, he had it transported to where it was needed, using every available means to do so. The workers used their cloaks to carry it and bundled it on the backs of the llamas. Soil was often carried great distances across mountains, canyons, and deserts.

The life of the *puric* was controlled down to the last detail and not a man or woman lived in the Inca's realm except as the Inca had decreed. The workers had no need to think for themselves about anything at all, not even their clothing. It was all arranged for them. Everyone could tell from far away which tribe a man belonged to, whether he was a Colla with a cap as round as a ball, or a Cañari who wore his hair plaited around his head, or a Huanca with braids which hung down to his knees. None of the workers needed to think. The Inca had charged other subjects to do the thinking, the "big-ears" in whose veins flowed Inca blood.

PICTURE FIVE: Here is one of the "big-ears," an *orejón;* supervising the construction of a bridge. A bridge was considered a part of a road which led to the presence of the Inca, that section of it which happened to hang in mid-air. It spanned the river from bank to bank and far below it the waters roared. If a bridge broke, the whole network of roads which held the Inca's empire together was disrupted. The bridges were the roads' little sisters. On all the roads and bridges there were couriers on the way to carry the Inca's commands to the outlying provinces. In this way, the Inca was everywhere at one and the same time, so to speak. Roads led through the desert and the bleak grasslands of the *puna*. They ran past snow-covered peaks, were tunneled through the living rock and along the steep banks of turbulent rivers. All along the line there were relay posts which the runners could rely on; there were storehouses, and places of rest which were known as *tampus*. If the ground was swampy there were broad raised causeways, and huge flights of steps where a mountain blocked the way. The roads were paved with *pirca*, a mixture of corn husks, mud, and pebbles. Ditches ran alongside the roads to drain them and there were often borders of *algarrobo* trees. Bridges and roads led everywhere, to every place which the Inca considered important, to the villages where gold was washed, and to signal posts near the glaciers. They ran from town to town and from one garrison to the next.

Without these roads the Spaniards might have found it impossible to invade the country. They crawled on all fours along the bridges which were made of fiber ropes and spanned the gorges. They found rivers which were bridged by no more than a single cable and where anyone who had to cross had no choice but to sit in a large basket cradle and swing over to the other side. The Spaniards did not trust these baskets in the least, but the Indians liked them. Runners, litter bearers, and whoever else traveled the Inca's roads in the old days looked forward to that part of the journey. It gave their feet a rest.

GOVERNADOR·DE·LOS·PVENTES·DESTE·RNO
CHACASVIOIOGACOSINGA
GVAMBOCHACA

All the news in those days was carried by runners who were called *chasquis*. They were housed at the relay stations, always ready to set off without a moment's delay, with their rations ready packed and a conch shell ready to blow, to announce their arrival at the next post.

These *chasqui* couriers were faster than horses and they would never disclose the messages they carried, even under torture. They ran straight on, regardless of snow, wind, or the heat of the desert, for no one might delay the Inca's communications, not even a prince.

The Inca considered himself the heart of his kingdom no matter where he might be, and not one of these rulers failed to build roads. Let me explain how this was achieved so quickly and without depriving the land of its agricultural workers. As soon as the Inca said, "A road will run from here to here," the civil engineers surveyed the territory and every community had to complete that section of the road which passed between its boundaries. When there was some special urgency, long convoys of extra helpers arrived, and they were often brought from far afield. With nothing more than copper tools and the use of fire and water, even walls of rock were pierced. Straight as a spear ran the Inca roads, thrusting far into the distance, and they were kept clean and tidy for the whole of their length so that nothing should offend the sight of the Inca when he traveled.

PICTURE SIX: The Inca was borne through the land in his golden litter. The *coya,* his queen, traveled with him. A canopy shaded them from the sun. The litter bearers were selected men who carried no one but the royal couple and they moved swiftly and silently on their way. They were men from the tribe of the Rucanas, who always provided litter bearers, just as the doctors were all drawn from the tribe of the Collahuis, the Cañaris supplied the Inca's bodyguard, and the Chumpivilcas were the court jesters and dancers. None of these needed to pay taxes, and neither did the craftsmen, weavers, goldsmiths, and potters, because their skill was valued so highly. Like the *puric,* they used only the simplest tools. The potter had no wheel, for the wheel in any form was quite unknown in ancient Peru.

These skilled craftsmen, however, were not among those who were entitled to wear gold disks in their ears. This privilege was granted to only two categories: to members of the Inca's family group and to the families of those princes who had been rulers in their own right before the Inca conquered their lands. Only the *orejones* could become court officials or governors, priests, and generals, yet even they

ANDASDELINGA
QVISPIRANPA

topa ynga yupanqui   mama ocllo coya

lleuan al ynga los y ñs callaua
ya españo
apaçcarse

pascare el ynga   como

dared do nothing on their own initiative. The Inca gave all the orders. We know of only one prince who went his own way; he was Otorongo, "The Tiger." He was sent on a campaign by Inca Roca, in order to punish jungle tribes who had been guilty of robbery and violence, and "The Tiger" decided to send his army home and to remain in the jungle himself. It was a unique incident, never to be repeated. Most officials wished to stay as close to the Inca's side as possible.

PICTURE SEVEN: The Inca's records were kept by means of long thick cords from which hung dozens of thinner strings with hundreds of knots in them. It was primarily a comprehensive bookkeeping system, but if my informants did not exaggerate, these cords, or *quipus,* as they were called, were also used as mnemonics to record laws, official announcements, and even poems.

Here is a *quipu* reader standing before the Inca, telling him what goods are stocked in the royal storehouses. The *camayoc* is shown here holding the main cord. It is stretched out and from it dangle the thinner threads, which were of different colors. It is as if he had opened the pages of a book. The Inca can read it too and apparently he has noticed some discrepancy. Pachacuti, the Inca who made all the school examinations more difficult, was particularly strict in training these *quipu* readers. "If a man cannot count these knots aright," he asked, "how can he count the stars?"

The Spaniards had nothing but contempt for these knotted cords. They tore them from the archives which were kept in Cuzco and all the other towns and burned them at the stake as "the Devil's strings" which tied the people to their false religion. But I, Poma, can testify that they were nothing of the kind. They were a system of stocktaking so that nothing could disappear from the warehouses, not even a pair of sandals. The fact was that Peru had a more highly organized system of orderly government than any Spaniard could possibly imagine!

This had not come about by chance. The reason for it was that all the highly placed officials had been rigorously trained for their jobs. The more exalted a man's rank, the more the Inca expected of him. The education of the princes and the sons of nobles was in the hands of the wise men, the *amautas,* and the Inca himself sometimes attended their classes. The main subjects taught in these schools were languages, religion, history, geography, and astronomy, and how to read the *quipus.*

The big examinations were held in public at the first feast of the year, the Inca Festival. They took place on the hill of

DEPOCITODELINGA
COLL CA

topaynga
yupanqui.

depoátes del ynga

Huanacauri, the place where the youngest brother of Manco
Capac had been turned to stone after serving the Sun God
for many years. The Inca and his court were all there, and
ten thousand paces away, the fourteen-year-old boys were
gathered, waiting for the great race. They had to run it uphill, through the thin air of the highland valley, and they
reached the summit panting for breath, where the prizes
were waiting for them. These consisted of figures made of
salt: falcons, wild ducks, hummingbirds, llamas, foxes, and
lizards—and there were snails for those who came in last.
The winners were awarded white trousers and the defeated
were given black ones. There was loud cheering for the good
runners and plenty of ridicule for the slowpokes. Each of the

76

competitors received a white cloak trimmed with black feathers.

After the race, there was a mock battle in which the boys had to show that they knew how to stand up to the enemy in time of war. Then, in front of the whole crowd, the youth had to demonstrate his practical ability. He had to make a pair of sandals and a spear, light a fire by rubbing two sticks together, and dig a row of holes for planting seeds in the earth. If a boy passed all his tests successfully he stepped before the Inca, who pierced his ears with a golden needle and gave him two golden ear disks to wear as a sign of the rank he had now earned. On the sacred terraces which ran around the Temple of the Sun, he received the insignia of his newly acquired noble rank from the elders of his clan. These were the shield and the mace, the spear and the sling. Finally the boys dived into the waters of the spring of Calipuqui, and then they were ready for whatever tasks in life the Inca would set them. There were no idlers, no leisured classes in the Inca's realm. The four school years concluded with an apprenticeship to one of the professions. And so the young *orejón* became a priest, an architect, or an officer, a civil engineer or an administrator, the servant of his supreme lord, the Inca.

PICTURE EIGHT: There was a separate school for the daughters of the nobility, called the *acllahuasi*. A few daughters of the *purics* were also admitted, but only those who had been specially selected after stringent tests by the Inca's representatives. These girls were trained for service in the temples and palaces. The Inca often presented them as a reward to members of his court, particularly to generals who had come back victorious from their wars. Some of these girls entered the King's harem. Others were trained in the rituals of the Sun, and were known as Virgins of the Sun. I, Poma de Ayala, had heard a great deal about their beauty, but in

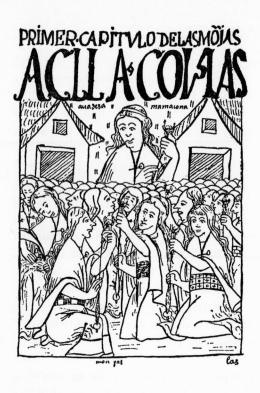

PRIMER·CAPITVLO·DELASMOÑAS
ACLLA·COÑAS

auadesa   mamacona

mon jas   las

my day these schools for the elect had already been abolished. So I fear that my pen must leave out many things, but at least I have made an attempt to portray the school as it was in the old days. The girls learned, among other things, how to spin, and the *mamacuna* who was in charge kept a strict eye on them. Even the daughters of the aristocracy with their wide belts and gold brooches, their robes and their flowing hair, are completely absorbed in their tasks, or else looking up anxiously in the hope that the *mamacuna* will be pleased with their work.

The *mamacuna* was always one of the Inca's sisters and she was the High Priestess, who drew sacred fire from the sun by means of a hollow golden mirror. She was the most im-

78

portant woman in the land after the *coya,* the queen. I have heard of queens who were as beautiful as the sun, who loved flowers and birds; but there were others, too, some of whom were drunkards or practiced witchcraft.

The *purics* placed great faith in the queen. They called her *Mamanchic,* "Our mother," and also *Huacha Cupac,* "Protector of the Unfortunate." Many of these queens are remembered still because they helped the people in time of war or disaster. Arequipa, a big city in the south, was once destroyed by an earthquake at a time when the Inca was away at the wars, and it was the *coya* who brought relief to the stricken city. And the *coya* of the tenth Inca ingeniously managed to find a way to spare the lives of a tribe who had rebelled against the state. The Inca had no choice in the matter. The state could not tolerate revolution and the rebels must die. Then the *coya* stepped in. She gave the tribe a new name, so that they were now the *yanacuna,* the "black servants," and the original tribe of the insurgents ceased to exist officially. The "black servants" did not appear in any records, but as it was the *coya* who had taken them under her wing, they could still carry on exactly as before and some of them were even promoted to posts of honor at the court. As the Daughter of the Sun, the *coya* was the symbol of life, not death.

PICTURE NINE: This shows the High Priest arrayed for a festival. He wears a headdress, his garments glow with rich colors, and he has golden bells at his knees and ankles. The pouch which he carries on his arm contains the knife used for making a sacrifice, and so he stepped toward the llama which he was about to dedicate to the sun. The llama was pure white, as unspotted as the god who gives life. The priest called on the heavens to look down and accept the sacrifice, whose blood was caught in a golden basin and offered to the creator of all life. The priest addressed the sun in these

79

words: "May you always remain as young as you were on the first day, giving light and warmth forever." The people joined in the prayer with cries of *"Hailli!"*

Sacrifices were made on various occasions. For instance, if a spring showed signs of drying up the priest would pray: "God, the source of all things, do not let this spring fail or there will be no harvest in the mountains." Llamas were offered up before a building was started and also at the time of sowing, to assure Pachamama, the earth mother, that these holes in her surface were not being bored with evil intent. Nothing could take place in the Inca world without invoking the participation of the heavens, and that is why the priests were of high rank. Only the Inca took precedence over the High Priest, the *Villac-Uma*.

One custom of the Incas astonished the Spaniards and that was the practice of confession among the people. There were special priests for this, who were known as the *Ichuri*, and anyone with a guilty conscience went to one of them. Sins included slander, malice aforethought, theft, adultery, conspiracy, and disobedience. In fact, there was a considerable list of misdemeanors. Confession had to take place on the banks of a river. The priest took a bunch of *ichu* grass in one hand and a stone in the other. He then took the sin upon himself, spat it into the tuft of grass, and threw it into the water so that the waves might carry it away. The sinner was given a blow with the stone and made to do penance. The most severe punishment was "to dwell in the wilderness." This meant spending a few days or even weeks entirely alone. The secrecy of the confessional was strictly kept by the priest.

Sin was regarded as something destructive, damaging not only to the transgressor but also to the regime. It was like siding against the Inca in the perpetual battle for good which he waged on behalf of the Sun God. The same was true of sickness. No matter what form it took, it must be speedily driven out. The priests who were responsible for healing were also magicians and doctors. Various medicines were used: quinine for fevers and wounds, wild barley for ulcers, condor's blood for nervous diseases, and bear's fat for tumors. Surgery was practiced and operations performed on the skull. In all kinds of illness, treatment aimed at exorcising the evil spirit who had caused the trouble, and the patient was always suspected of having sinned in some way. If he recovered, he was warned not to do it again! The basic rule of life went like this: *Ama sua, ama llulla, ama cheklla*— Do not steal, do not lie, do not be lazy! Whoever offended against it insulted both the Inca and the Sun God.

PICTURE TEN: The worst crime which anyone could commit was conspiracy against the Inca. For this threw doubt on the fact that the Incas were indeed the Sons of the Sun. In such a case, the Inca left it to the heavens to punish the culprit. He was thrown into a dungeon which he had to share with snakes and jaguars for two days and two nights. If the man was still alive on the third day, he was allowed to go free.

Any man who assaulted a Virgin of the Sun was shown no mercy. He and his whole family with him were exterminated. Anyone who sabotaged bridges or storehouses, who cut down fruit trees or killed llamas also paid the penalty with his life. There was severe punishment for anyone who worked the fields of the *camayoc* when he should have been attending to those of the Inca or the Sun God, but a man caught stealing food was given extra land in order to satisfy his hunger. Everyone was entitled to receive what he needed to maintain life. For this reason there was an order prohibiting the shelling of corn kernels, and the word went: If those who shelled corn had enough sense, they would surely weep as they did it, for they are simply cheating themselves.

The Inca not only watched over his people but protected wild life too, especially guanacos and vicuñas. In each district a great roundup was held in every fourth year and as many as twenty thousand Indians would take part, making an enormous ring to close in on the animals. Guanacos were usually killed on these occasions, but the vicuñas were clipped and allowed to go free. It was from this vicuña wool that clothes were made for the Inca and the nobility, for it can be woven into cloth as light and smooth as silk. If anyone killed a vicuña or took the wool for his own use, he was made to lie on the ground and a heavy stone was dropped onto his shoul-

Suspension bridge across a canyon. Apurimac region
(Next pages)
Machu Picchu, seen from the peak of Huayna Picchu

82

CASTIGO INSTICIA
SAVICAHINOVICIO

yaya pachacamac
uanazacyay
cay son cuy
payuyas
can mi

cay pacchoyayam
ma uarcanquima
ma uacyauar
can qui

zancay
sulla mi
cuuay huoga
zapa son cuyta

may pim
canquihu
chaza papa
camachic qui
pichiuayruna
cama dios

castigo   castigos

ders. There again, chance was allowed to play a part in whether the miscreant survived or not.

PICTURE ELEVEN: When it was sowing time, the fields of the Sun God had first priority. The Inca himself was present, and he took the pointed digging stick in his own hands and stood in line with the common laborers. This was a feast day for him and he stuck flowers in his scarlet headband. The men broke up the earth with their foot plows and the women planted the seed in time to the sacred songs. First the men sang:

Intihuatana, the "Stone of the Sun." Machu Picchu

Ayau hailli, ayau hailli!
Kapai Inti, Apu Yaya,
Kaway kuri, sumay kuri.
Great Sun, mighty father,
Wake the seeds and make them grow.

Then the women answered:

Hailli, Pachamama, hailli!
Hailli, oh Earth Mother, *hailli!*

So the land was tilled at the command of the Sun and with the co-operation of Mother Earth. Without these two, nothing could thrive.

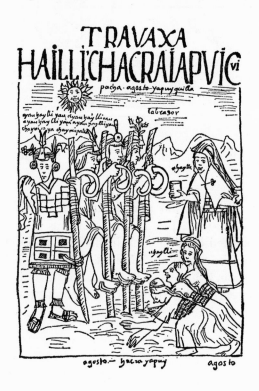

The Sun had arranged the year in the best possible way. In the middle of it came the Festival of the Sun, the *Inti Raymi*. The Festival of the Inca, the *Capac Raymi*, was held at the beginning of the year, and the twelve months were named after the chief feasts which occurred in each of them. After *Capac Raymi* came the Small Ripening, and then the Great Ripening. There followed the Garment of Flowers, the Dance of the Young Corn, the Song of the Harvest, the Festival of the Sun, and the Earthly Purification. Then came the Great Purification, the Feast of the Queen, the Festival of the Waters, and finally, the Procession of the Dead.

At the onset of the rainy season, a festival was held to drive away all illnesses. Any strangers in the town and all those who were sick were sent away for the day. The healthy ones rubbed their faces with cooked corn, lit torches, and brandished their weapons of war as if invisible enemies had to be put to flight. They shook their cloaks over the streams and rivers and the waves carried the sickness away. For it was the Inca's wish that there should be no darkness in all the earth, and this the people were told by the priests.

The priests of highest rank were also astronomers. On the day of the solstice, they "bound" the sun against a pillar cut out of the living rock. The priests had devised a calendar and they knew all about the equinox. They could predict the time of noon when an upright column casts no shadow. In Quito, a city near the equator, "the Sun God was enthroned on his tower in a great blaze of light." The sun drove away the darkness from the sky; the Inca dispelled it from the earth. Sun and Inca were one. When an Inca died, he did not cease to be with his people. He took part in their festivals even after his death—that is, as a mummy, which is *malqui* in the Inca language, "a tree which bears fruit." At the Feast of the Sun, the *malqui* sat near the living Inca on a throne of rock and had a part in the ceremonial sacrifices. The *malqui*

85

were there to keep watch and to see that everything in the kingdom happened just as the Sun God had ordained.

PICTURE TWELVE: The Inca's realm was the Kingdom of the Sun. Not only temples were built in his honor but whole cities. Cuzco, where the Inca lived, was especially dedicated to him. It was divided into twelve districts which had charming names: Hummingbird, Lizard, Salt Window, Tobacco Field, and the like. Certain quarters were allocated to different social groups: for instance, the aristocracy, the craftsmen, and the common people. Other areas were set aside for granaries or for the royal residences.

In the middle of the town sparkled a great house of gold. Like all the other buildings, it was thatched, except that here and there strands of gold were woven in among the straw. Cuzco was a symbol of the sun's realm, hemmed in by mountains, built in a valley close to the sky, the embodiment of the Inca's might.

The Inca people saw Cuzco as the sacred animal, the puma. Between the roaring torrents of its two rivers, the Huatenay and the Tullumayo, lay its body. Vilcamayu was its tail, and the fortress of Sacsahuamán the head. The oldest palaces were made of huge blocks of stone; the later ones had walls in which all the stones were exactly alike. There were three hundred and thirty *huacas* or shrines in and around Cuzco, and on one height outside the town a great gateway made of rock reached toward the sky. For the Incas made the rock serve them too. They took it and formed it according to their will. They built walls from it, and dams and altars. The finest of the Inca buildings were made of stone. The Sons of the Sun built a house for their nation on which the sun could shine down peacefully. Their kingdom was indeed great and the Incas were good rulers. I, Felipe Huamán Poma de Ayala, say so.

86

AMOjONADORESDESTEREiNO.
MVACAVCHO.COMARAQVI
INGA   INGA

Sarmiento the Sailor's Verdict: I, Pedro Sarmiento de Gamboa, say that the Incas were bad rulers. The Viceroy of Peru assigned to me the task of discovering how the people of Peru lived while these Sons of the Sun reigned. We Spaniards have often been represented as devils who brought all kinds of misery to the natives of Peru, but I know that we freed them from slavery. I have conducted hearings throughout the land and I am in a position to say just what despots these Incas really were. They were tyrants who exploited their own people and the many subject tribes as well. Their kingdom was large for the simple reason that other sovereign states had been conquered to make it so, and countless human lives had been sacrificed too. The Incas had drums made out of the skins of their enemies. In Cuzco, a whole charnel house was filled with skulls which had been taken as trophies in battle. In the conquered lands, many a field lay soaked in blood, many lagoons were dyed red, many a hill was a mound of the slain.

When Manco Capac invaded the Valley of Cuzco with his Inca tribe, he did not come as a teacher and benefactor. The people living there already had a system of agriculture; they had their own temples and towns. Manco Capac came as an oppressor, who stole their land and killed everyone who would not yield. Even the Inca women fought with the men. On the terraced salt fields near Cuzco, the descendants of the defeated tribesmen told me that Mama Ocllo herself had ripped the lungs from the breast of a man and had blown them up with her own breath. Terrified at such savagery, the natives had fled.

At no time did the Incas shrink from fratricide. One of the original four Inca brothers was murdered by the other three. Pachacuti slew his brother Yupanqui. Atahualpa had his brother Huáscar brutally assassinated. Nor was their piety worth very much either. One Inca terrified his priests by asking them if they really believed that the sun could be a god when, day after day, he covered the same course, no better than an animal led by the rope? Atahualpa killed a priest with a golden ax, because he had prophesied that the Inca would die young.

No one could trust this last of the Incas, who admitted himself that he had intended to kill every Spaniard except one. He would save only the smith, from whom he hoped to wrest the secret of manufacturing iron. These Incas told everyone the same lie, that they had been appointed to rule by the Sun God for the benefit of mankind. But what, may I ask, did mankind mean to them? The people were mere tools which the rulers could manipulate according to their

88

will. In the Inca's kingdom, only the emperor counted. The rest of the population were so many heads to be counted.

From the farthest corners of the kingdom came the census takers and woe to the *curaca* who might be discovered hiding a child in a cave in order to evade taxation. He would be brought to justice without mercy. Tribute was demanded not only in goods, in corn and wool, in llamas and in metals, but also in human form. A man could be forced to serve as a runner, a litter bearer, or a temple servant, and even to become a human sacrifice.

Everyone's place in life was decided for him by the Inca. He might be sent away from his home to go to war, or to build roads and terraces in some distant part of the country. Or he and all his family might be resettled in a strange neighborhood. But if he was not made to leave his home the alternative was just as bad. He was tied to his plot of land his whole life long and was not allowed to leave it. Year after year he tilled the same fields in the same village, sometimes his own but more often those of others, plowing the fields of the Sun or of the Inca or perhaps those of a neighbor who had been called up for service. His only pleasures were to get drunk on *chicha* when the feast days came round, to lick the cakes of salt provided by the state, or to gamble with beans like everyone else in the village.

The people were not allowed even to eat what they liked. They had to take all their meals at the open door to prove that no one was gorging himself on meat while everyone else had to put up with corn broth. No delicacies were allowed and people who were dirty were made to eat dirt. Every hut had to look exactly like the next one, every workman like all the others. Decorations of feathers or the use of vicuña wool were reserved for the aristocracy. The laborer went about in a much-mended shift, using the most primitive tools for his work, which went on without respite. For the Inca took good care that everyone had his hands fully occupied. Huayna

SESTA CALLE
CORO·TASQVE

Capac said to his sons, "If you can find nothing else for the people to do, then get them to shift a mountain. If you keep them busy you will have peace in your realm."

The Incas banned the workers' sons forever from the schools, for otherwise the lowly might get ideas above their station. But even the generals, the Lords of Ten Thousands, yes, even "The Four" between whom the rule of the four quarters of the kingdom was shared, did not dare to decide anything for themselves, not even when their ruler was a captive in Cajamarca. The last Inca, Atahualpa, had so terrorized his subjects that they thought of him as a volcano

Earthenware jug in the shape of a frog found in the Nazca Valley. Nazca style

pouring forth fire, or as an avalanche which could bury whole villages. It was only when we Spaniards came that the spell was lifted. Many subject tribes welcomed us as liberators, for they remembered how life had looked before the Incas conquered them. I may not have been among the first of my fellow countrymen to arrive in Peru, but still I, Sarmiento the Sailor, tell you plainly that these Incas were never the Sons of the Sun.

Here is an extract from the report of the officer, Sierra de Leguisamo, the one who came with Pizarro and gambled away the sun before it rose: The King of Spain can take my word that when we came to the land of the Incas, order prevailed everywhere. There was no such thing as theft or idleness or blasphemy. We have taken away much from these people and what is worse, we have corrupted them. The Incas must have been wise rulers, for during their reign there was little crime. According to old custom it was sufficient to place a bunch of feathers before an open door to show that a house was empty, and no one would dream of entering. But we Spaniards forced our way into their houses and into their holy places. There was only one town in the whole dominion which did not fall into our hands, and that was the capital of the rebel Incas, the seven who were Incas in name only. Theirs was only a phantom kingdom with a handful of loyal subjects. In spite of all our searching, we never discovered the lost city.

A crouching figure with a wrinkled face. Mochica pottery, found in the Chicama Valley

The lost city

At the edge of the great forests, below the ice-covered peaks, the rebel Inca, Manco Capac II, found a safe hiding place for himself three years after the death of Atahualpa. For four hundred years this city remained a mystery, sealed off from the world, until Hiram Bingham set out to find it and did so.

Bingham was leading an expedition from Yale University when, on July 24, 1911, he discovered the remains of Machu Picchu, the rebel residence. Many others before him had tried to find it, conquerors, adventurers, treasure seekers, and explorers, but all had had to give up in the end and many of them, exhausted by the long quest, had doubted if the city had ever existed. But it must have done so once, since Spanish records in Peru at the time mention a hiding place to which Manco Capac II, whom Pizarro had enthroned as a puppet Inca, escaped from the Spaniards with his court, his treasure, his priests, and a small army. He and his followers were declared outlaws and for forty years, despised by the Spaniards, they dwelt in the wilderness. The Inca army made all roads north of Cuzco unsafe for travelers, and the puppet Inca captured prisoners. Some Spaniards went over to his side and various negotiators who were sent out with instructions to try to come to terms with the Inca actually approached his capital.

Hiram Bingham knew all this before he started, for he was a professor of history who had studied the period. But perhaps after four hundred years, there would be nothing left of the lost capital. It might have fallen into ruin so that every trace had been obliterated. All the same, Bingham was optimistic. Inca cities do not vanish so easily. They were built to endure and even earthquakes do not destroy them. The town which for forty long years was the focus of Indian resistance to the conquerors of Peru could not have disappeared completely, of that Bingham felt certain. It was simply that the rebels had concealed themselves exceptionally well in some obscure corner which no one had as yet discovered. All the forces of nature, the ice-covered mountains, the turbulent rivers, the jungle, and the naked rock, had conspired to bar the way to any would-be invader.

Two years after the discovery, the geographer attached to the expedition made this statement: "Our expedition has discovered a territory of about 1,800 square miles of whose existence no one was aware before 1911. Although it is only one hundred miles from Cuzco, it seems to be one of the largest unrecorded glacier regions in South America, and it is difficult to see how the last of the Incas could have found a better refuge."

In his search for the Inca town, Bingham met many dangers and difficulties. There were bears, vampire bats, and many snakes. He and his companions came to rivers which could rise thirteen feet in a matter of hours, rivers which had cut canyons through the rock to a depth of 2,300 feet. Jungle vapors steamed from these gorges and clouds of insects hovered around the heads of the intruders. In the thick undergrowth they saw centipedes, salamanders, poisonous spiders, and snakes which laid traps for their victims. They dared to enter a world which did not permit a single careless step. But it was only here that there was any prospect of stumbling on the lost city. The rest of Peru had been thoroughly combed by the Spaniards. The more the territory was hostile to mankind, the more promising it was for Bingham's purpose. If the lost Inca city had not been found after four centuries of searching, then it must be in a locality where everyone else considered it was impossible for a town to exist, in some region which looked inaccessible. Below Salcantay, the wild mountain, in the shadow of twenty-thousand-foot peaks, above the Urubamba River, Bingham found such a place, cut off from the rest of the world by precipitous walls of rock well over two thousand feet high.

Bingham had already discovered some Inca ruins on this expedition. He had found "the town where gold is washed" and also the remains of Chopaquirau, a city that had commanded the upper Apurimac Valley. There used to be a suspension bridge over a hundred yards long across the river, and a Spaniard who had been there soon after the Conquest admitted that the bridge with the wild torrent rushing below it had terrified him. This bridge which spanned the water from rock to rock seemed to be lost in the roar of the waters below, for this was the River Apurimac, where the Great Speaker had his shrine. Pedro Sancho described it as he saw it: "The image stood by the bridge in a painted niche. It had breasts like a woman's and a massive belt of gold. It sat on a stout beam, which was thicker than a fat man, and whenever the Inca visited the shrine, the god spoke with him."

Hiram Bingham knew of this report, for a Peruvian scholar had drawn his attention to it. There were other records too, in which there was mention of some hiding place of the Inca's. The idea of these rebels seemed to rankle in the

94

mind of the Spanish Viceroy, and he kept sending out soldiers in attempts to take the Inca prisoner. They reported
back that their efforts had been fruitless, but in their bulletins two names kept recurring, those of Vitcos and Vilcabamba. There was a reference too to "a white stone . . .
above a spring by the place called Chuquipulca, where there
was a temple to the sun." All these places lay in narrow
gorges between the Urubamba and the Apurimac rivers, a
few hundred miles from Cuzco.

One of the roads running north from the Salt Window sector of the Inca capital led past some ancient citadels into the
Vilcabamba region, into a land of huge, ice-covered peaks, a
world of orchids, of hummingbirds, and of raging torrents.
Bingham decided to set off along this road, following the
russet waters of the river which became the Urubamba. He
sought until he found a white wall of rock above a spring
near which there were ruined houses. In them he found remains of the Spaniards: horseshoes, saddle gear, a Jew's-
harp, and rusty scissors. He penetrated into the jungle valley of Pampaconas, still on the trail which the Spaniards had
left for him, and which must have gone back to the times of
the last Inca or not very much later. He came upon many
white stones, but they did not help him much. In 1875,
Charles Wiener had noted in his diary that he had heard of
ruins not far from Mount Machu Picchu; and on a map
drawn some years before by the Peruvian explorer Raimondi,
a peak named Machu Picchu was entered between the two
rivers, the Apurimac and the Urubamba. So Raimondi had
known about the mountain, although the city of the same
name had eluded him.

The most conclusive evidence for Bingham's theory, however, was contained in the "Report of Diego Rodríguez de
Figuroa on his dealings with the Inca Titu Cusa Yupanqui
in the Andes of Vilcabamba"—that is, somewhere in the
neighborhood of the lost city. Titu Cusa, the last Inca but

one, had had dealings with Diego," the bearded little man,"
in a village called Puquinra and the Inca had shown himself
more than a match for the Viceroy's emissary. Another road
was also mentioned in the report, "one which leads to Sapa-
marca and Picchu." The constant repetition of that name, in
the old Spanish records, in Raimondi's map, and in Wiener's footnote, strengthened Bingham's resolve. He circled
the base of Machu Picchu; he asked questions of everyone living in the area; and a planter also made inquiries for him
throughout the district. The information he gleaned decided him to continue along the Urubamba by canoe.

Then Bingham met a man named Melchor Arteaga, who

Plan of Machu Picchu (according to Bingham, Machu Picchu,
A Citadel of the Incas, *London, 1930): 1. City gateway 2.
Terraced fields for crops 3. Well 4. Living quarters for one
of the many* ayllus *(clans) 5. Temple square and "House of
the Three Windows" 6. Intihuatana ("Stone of the Sun") 7.
The foot of Huayna Picchu 8. Semicircular temple 9 and
10. Living quarters for various clans 11 and 12. Squares with
tombs*

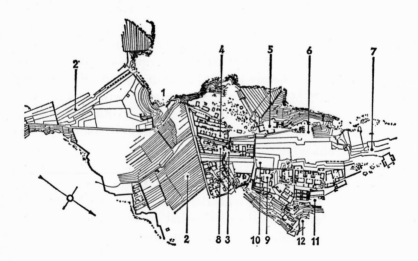

actually knew of ruins near the peak of Machu Picchu. Bingham's companions gave little weight to Arteaga's information. Worn out by the long weeks of fruitless searching, they pitched camp by the banks of the Urubamba and stayed there. One of them wanted to collect butterflies; another had to wash his shirts. And so, on the morning of July 24, Bingham set off accompanied by Arteaga and a Peruvian, Sergeant Carrasco. They crossed the swift river by the rickety footbridge, but when they began to climb the mountain, the ascent soon grew very difficult. Often they had to scramble on hands and knees through dense undergrowth, and steep cliffs hampered their progress. Arteaga, who was not as stoutly shod as the sergeant, was nervous about snakes. The precipice rose sheer above them, straight toward the noonday sun. Far below them was the noisy white ribbon of river, and on the other side of it reared the northern face of the canyon, naked gray stone which towered to the sky, as lifeless as a slice of the moon's surface.

The three men kept gasping for breath as they crawled on all fours to make a path through the wilderness. Then, quite unexpectedly, they saw two grass huts a little way away and the friendly faces of two Indians who had fresh water in water carriers with them. They were delighted to see visitors and offered the explorers something to drink. They said that their names were Álvarez and Richarte, and showed Bingham and his companions into their huts. They grew corn on the hillside, as well as sweet potatoes, sugar cane, tomatoes, beans, and gooseberries. Their fields were unusually narrow and each strip of land stood one step higher than the next, rising up the steep slope like a staircase. They must be Inca terraces, thought Bingham. They were absolutely typical, like the ones at Pisac. His tiredness vanished. He asked about ruins. Álvarez pointed to the saddle between two peaks above them and offered them his son as a guide.

The lad led the way, gliding between the thorny bushes

and bamboos. Suddenly a white wall gleamed through the jungle and then wherever Bingham turned there were walls and more terraces. He stared at the miracle of hewn stone and whispered, "I must be dreaming."

They stood there on the saddle between "Young" Picchu and "Old" Picchu, with the river seething below, surrounded by the snow-covered peaks. On this saddle a whole town had been built, a city in the clouds, a human eyrie. They were long-forgotten, abandoned Inca terraces on which Álvarez and Richarte had planted their corn.

Bingham, who was familiar with Inca buildings, could tell at once that these were Inca walls before his eyes. One wall which he saw was magnificent. "There isn't another to equal it in the whole of Peru," he declared. And one stone he discovered had not merely twelve angles like the world-famous stone of Cuzco, but thirty-two. Bingham saw Cyclopean foundations made of square blocks weighing several tons each, and wherever he looked there were flights of steps. But everything was overgrown, strangled beneath the growth of jungle. Bingham determined he would clear it all away.

He and his two companions looked down toward the river. It rushed past like a swift endless snake, two thousand feet below them. The water enclosed the city on three sides and the fourth side was barred by a high ridge. Now they could understand how the town had remained hidden for centuries. It was not far from Cuzco, and once there must have been secret paths connecting the two cities, but unless you knew them, the broken bridges across the river put an end to one's quest. Except for the initiated, the city did not exist. But it must have been abandoned long ago, Bingham knew. It was a dead city, buried beneath the tangled creepers.

The following year, Hiram Bingham returned to Machu Picchu to awaken "his" town to a new life. Again he led an expedition and he persuaded ten Indians to accompany them, but he had much difficulty with them on the site. The only willing native helper was Tomás Cobinas, a member of the Civil Guard.

The first task was to build a bridge over the Urubamba which would stretch from one side of the canyon to the other. This they did by using cables, for they had brought suitable equipment with them and so were able to outwit the river, their most formidable obstacle. When they reached Machu Picchu, they cleared away the jungle with machetes and with fire. They had to cart away the debris bit by bit, blackened creepers, roots, and heaps of earth, working away patiently until eventually they brought to light what human hands had achieved. For four whole months every corner of the town was investigated as it was uncovered and the surrounding districts were explored as well. This was not without its dangers. Eight poisonous snakes were killed in the first week alone and two of the pack mules died from snake bites. One of Bingham's men, Heald, tried to climb "Young" Picchu by following a bear's trail. He almost fell and it was with a sprained arm that he managed to reach the peak, at his third attempt.

Bingham sent out Indians to look for caves. The first group found none, but another search party discovered eight

Emergency bridge over the Urubamba

in one day. They knew what to look for, and all together more than fifty caves were found which had once served as burial places and were now the haunt of bear and jaguar. Beyond the mountain saddle, Bingham found tombs from which the dead looked down on the town as it came to life again after its long sleep. But the jungle did not let it go without a struggle. Three times during the four months of excavation the site had to be cleared, but by August 1912 the jungle was defeated and the town of Machu Picchu was won for the archaeologists.

One of the most striking features of the city was the great flight of terraces which had once been sown with corn and other crops and was now visible for the first time since the days of the Incas. Opposite them were a variety of buildings to be seen, some with their walls built of huge unhewn blocks, some with walls of the finest Inca workmanship, and others which had been very hastily erected. Everywhere there were flights of stairs, over one hundred of them. One member of the expedition tried to count the steps but he gave up at 3,200. The biggest flight of all cut through the center of the town, and two others at right angles to it divided the town into quarters. Side by side were big houses with gardens and humble dwellings. A stairway hewn out of one single block led to the only well. In the middle of the town was the Field of the Sun, a square surrounded by temples. Some of the walls were of pale granite with windows and niches in trapezoid form. There was a semicircular tower and beneath it was a cave with a throne and alcoves skillfully carved. Close by rose that lightly poised wall which, for Bingham, was the most beautiful in the whole of Peru. And not far from this wall was a house with three windows, an incomparable building made of white andesite.

In the middle of the square with the granite temples lay a huge stone with a snake carved on it, a *huaca*. There were more of these sacred stones scattered about the city. Straight

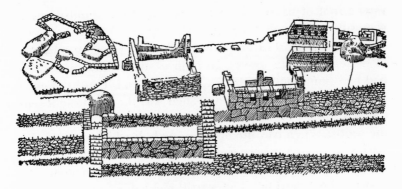

Part of Machu Picchu with the "House of the Three Windows"
and huacas *(sacred stones)*

above the abyss, where the cliffs fell sheer to the Urubamba, a daring flight of steps led upward to a stone that was "bound to the sun." It was a column carved out of the living rock and its shadow was the hand of the clock which marked the solar year.

Below a rock face one hundred feet high, Bingham found the grave of a woman in which were a hollow bronze mirror and shreds of cotton garments. She was probably a priestess. It was not unusual for women to be buried in tombs apart from the men. When Manco Capac fled from the Spaniards, many of the Virgins of the Sun fled with him, and here in the lost city the Inca and his subjects lived the lives they were used to. They sacrificed to the sun and enjoyed the fruits of the earth by which they lived. At night they wrapped themselves in their cloaks and slept on the bare earth. The terraced fields kept them from starvation and the jungle winds carried enough moisture to make the crops grow. It was a hanging city nourished by its hanging fields and independent of outside sources, and that was how the rebel headquarters survived, close to the glaciers and the jungle but an impregnable fortress. A mat before the doorway, a roof of straw, a hearth, and a few household utensils were sufficient for their needs.

Inside the houses were found five times as many splinters of pottery as in the graves, an indication that Machu Picchu had had numerous inhabitants until the end. Until the end? But when had that occurred? When was the last time a sentry was posted to safeguard the town from an attack from the south? When had the heavy stone bolt which secured the town's only gateway been shot for the last time?

Hiram Bingham and his team searched for evidence to answer the question. The earth yielded many fragments from the late Inca period, about two hundred little objects, mainly of bronze, with only a few of tin or silver, such as mirrors, rings, pendants, bracelets, bells, and axes. There was no gold. It suggested that everything of greater value had been removed. But why was the stronghold abandoned if the Spaniards never found it?

Bingham thought the answer lay in the water supply.

Pottery fragments from the late Inca period (according to Bingham, Machu Picchu, A Citadel of the Incas, *London, 1930)*

There was only one well. In the four months during which Machu Picchu was being excavated, it yielded barely enough water for fifty men. Did the source start drying up four hundred years ago? If so, then the loyal subjects of the Inca had had no choice but to leave. But by then perhaps they had already realized that further resistance was useless.

For forty long years the oppressed people tried to shake off the yoke of the Spaniards. At first, the conquerors had nominated a grandson of Atahualpa's to reign and they had conceded him the name of the first Inca, Manco, but they gave him no power. The Inca fled, but he was recaptured. Then he tricked his guards, who included one of Pizarro's brothers, and escaped a second time. Not much later, however, at the beginning of April 1536, he came back of his own accord and appeared before Cuzco—at the head of an Inca army. The time was well chosen, for a considerable portion of the Spanish army was away on a campaign in Chile and others were seeking their fortune in different parts of the country. Pizarro was miles away, occupied with the founding of Lima near the sea. The whole of Peru was ablaze, the people were rising. Lima was besieged, but most of the Indian forces were concentrated on Cuzco.

The Inca army dug trenches and spiked them with sharpened stakes. They took Spanish prisoners and forced them to supply them with gunpowder and to teach them how to use firearms. They rode the horses they had captured. In rags, embittered, starving, robbed of their lands, but still very apt pupils of the Spaniards in all the arts of war, they were out to avenge Atahualpa who had been strangled to death and to punish the Spaniards who had debased the natives to the level of pack animals. They fought like wounded jaguars.

They scorched the earth around Cuzco and the old Inca capital went up in flames. After seven days, only one hundred and thirty-six Spaniards survived and half of them were wounded. Their end seemed inevitable, yet they did not surrender. They had observed that Manco fought for only seven days in each month, that is, as long as the moon was in its first quarter. Then for three weeks he would leave the beleaguered garrison in peace. The Spaniards used this breathing space to go over to the attack, and although they were very cruel they met with little resistance. They kept breaking through and crushing the ranks of the besiegers, and this went on for many months.

Manco's men had dug themselves into the fortress of Sacsahuamán, behind its triple zigzag walls with their great blocks of stone. Juan Pizarro was one of those who tried to storm it, but a stone from a sling struck him on the head and he was killed. In the end, however, the Spaniards forced their way into the citadel. The last turret was defended by an old Inca prince. When he saw that he was the sole survivor, he wrapped his cloak around him and threw himself into the ravine below.

Manco Capac promptly besieged the fortress and the situation for the Spaniards seemed more desperate than ever. Then suddenly, on February 16, 1537, the Inca army withdrew. The soldiers had to go home to sow the corn, for there was an even older enemy than the Spaniards to drive from their country—famine. The puppet Inca had to flee. At Ollantaytambo he threw his army against the Spanish once more and his son was taken prisoner. He himself escaped with his court, his llama herds, and the mummies of some of his ancestors, and found some hiding place which the Spaniards never discovered.

The Viceroy posted a garrison in the area, and a captain was sent out to bring the Inca back. Exhausted after riding through trackless country, the officer with his twenty men suddenly came upon the Inca, at the head of his troops, riding one of the four horses he had captured. Only six Spaniards were able to escape. The heads of the others were tossed over the garrison wall during the night.

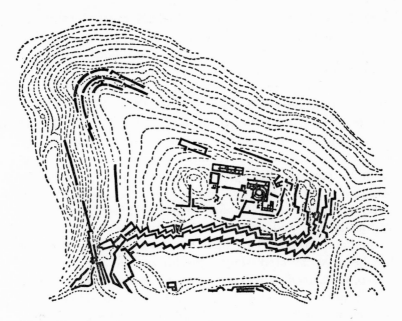

Plan of Sacsahuamán

In 1542, the six Spaniards who had managed to save their lives went over to Manco Capac. Two years later, after certain laws had been passed to protect the Indians, the Viceroy thought that it was a good moment to try to arrange a settlement with the Inca. So he offered the deserters a free pardon if they would persuade the Inca to agree to a treaty. These six men were having a game of skittles when a quarrel arose between them and their hosts, and one Spaniard flung a ball so hard at the Inca's head that the emperor fell dead. That put negotiations out of the question for some time. Meanwhile, hatred of the *conquistadores* had grown so great that the next Inca himself fell a victim to it. He was poisoned because he was considering a treaty with the Spaniards. The Viceroy sent out one bloodhound after another to track down the secret hide-out, but the town remained a mystery.

And the rebels went on with their stubborn resistance. They made the roads unsafe, they cut down bridges, they captured horses—and Spaniards. For several decades, the viceroys could only look on helplessly. Then, in 1571, Friar Gavriel de Oviedo offered to seek out the Inca Tupac Amaru and talk to him. The friar came to the resthouse of Cocha Cajas and then to Huampu, but he had to turn back when he reached the Apurimac River, for the suspension bridge had been destroyed. He returned to Cuzco in order to try again, this time choosing to go via Ollantaytambo, the Panticalla Pass, and across the Urubamba to the headwaters of the Pampaconas. There he succeeded in meeting the Inca, but he never entered Machu Picchu and he came back to Cuzco, unharmed, it is true, but alone and without a treaty.

The next year, Captain García, a cousin of Ignatius of Loyola, was sent out by the viceroy on the trail of Tupac Amaru. García, who was married to a niece of the Inca, at last succeeded in tracking down his quarry and it was he who captured Tupac Amaru. He brought him back to Cuzco where the Viceroy had him beheaded. The people watched the execution in silence, but at night they came and knelt before the decapitated head which had been stuck on a pole by order of the Viceroy. He had to have it removed.

The Inca drama was all over. The capital in the desert had no meaning any more. It became "the lost city," until Hiram Bingham discovered it.

At least, Bingham was convinced that this was it, for there were so many fragments and remains which belonged to the last Inca period and Inca walls like those which stood in Cuzco. There was that magnificent house, too, the one with the three windows, which was pure Inca architecture. When

(Above) Jar in the form of a head. Nazca pottery
(Below) Tortoise lying on its back. Nazca pottery

Bingham saw it he recalled the old chronicles through which he had browsed and an excerpt from one of them came to his mind:

"Manco Capac, the first Inca, ordered a house to be built with three windows. It was to be erected at the place of his birth and in memory of that cave from which he had once emerged."

There was a cave in Machu Picchu in which there stood an altar or a throne with wonderfully carved niches around it. But even more important, nowhere else in Peru was there a more beautiful three-windowed palace, and Bingham was convinced that he had found not only the last but also the first Inca city.

He went on digging. He found walls in Machu Picchu which were different from Inca walls, Cyclopean structures which were similar to those found elsewhere in the highlands of Peru, often as foundations for Inca buildings. Who had carried these blocks of stone weighing many tons to these heights? Why, it was difficult enough to climb the mountains unladen.

Fresh riddles confronted Bingham. The more deeply he dug, the more finds he made which dated back to the earliest times: stone axes, bison bones, strangely shaped pieces of wood and bone, and so many obsidian cubes that they would seem to have fallen as meteorites. He unearthed obsidian knives and objects in forms which had never been found in other Inca cities and vessels with patterns copied from the jungle around it, for the jungle was always Machu Picchu's sinister neighbor. In those four months at Bingham's disposal he found many objects which were very old indeed.

Bingham also examined the oldest parts of the walls of Ollantaytambo, the town which stood between Machu Picchu and Cuzco. Their defenses were turned *against* Cuzco,

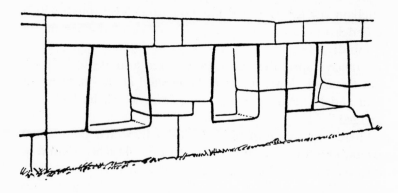

"The Three Windows"

so that it was hardly likely the town was built by those kings who lived in Cuzco. Had it been built by the Kingdom of the Giants, of which there were legends long before the Inca empire was founded? Bingham believed so, and he thought that the foundations of Machu Picchu went back into prehistory, to the time when there was a kingdom called Pirua governed by the Amauta kings, who showed the people of the Andes how to plant corn, how to make tools and pottery, and how to build cities.

For Bingham, Machu Picchu was a city in which nature and human handiwork went hand in hand, a throne for gods and men. It awakened dreams in him which were, perhaps, romantic, but that did not prevent him from observing and recording his findings with the greatest precision, and he did not conceal anything, not even one find which was in danger of robbing him of his reputation as a discoverer. On his first day in Machu Picchu, on that twenty-fourth of July, 1911, he had come across a stone on which a Spanish name was scrawled and the date 1902. So nine years before, someone else had been there, had scratched his name on a wall, and had gone away, telling no one of the hidden city and so leaving the field open for Bingham to claim its discovery.

Machu Picchu, like Cuzco, was made of stone. Indeed, all the towns and fortresses in the highlands were built of granite. But roads from the mountains led down to the coast, where there were other towns, built before the Inca brothers had climbed through their three windows. These coastal cities, however, were made of mud bricks, and they were built by men whose appearance was quite different from that of the Incas and who lived quite different lives.

As one by one they were subdued by the Inca's armies and ordered to worship the sun as their chief god in future, their priests said, "We have our own deity, the moon, which brings

Fragment of pottery (Tiahuanaco) from the time of the Amauta kings

us life from the sea, and he is better than the sun. The moon gives us fish and makes our fields grow. But the earth dies beneath the glare of the sun."

The coastal tribes were called the Yuncas. Their world lay buried beneath the dry sand and so their remains have been preserved much better than those in the highlands. The deeper the archaeologists dug beneath the loose earth, the more amazing were their finds. True, they came across traces of the treasure seekers, the *conquistadores* and the Incas. But from the deepest strata there came to light remains of the Yunca world proper, pottery, textiles, and metalwork in a richness and variety unknown anywhere else in Peru. In the sands of the desert, the scholars found the footprints of the pyramid builders; they discovered kingdoms which had been wholly submerged and forgotten.

The kingdoms
of the coast

Baltasar Martínez Compañon, a former Bishop of Trujillo, is usually considered to be Peru's first archaeologist. He lived approximately two hundred years ago, and wherever he went he searched for evidence of past history.

On the outskirts of Trujillo there lay a strip of desert about eight square miles in area which was covered with ruined walls. The Bishop had read the chronicles of the conquerors and Indian princes, and he knew that on this spot had stood a great city, Chan-Chan, the capital of the Chimus. He began to take measurements and estimated that many of the walls must have been nearly thirty feet high. He proved that when the city was founded it must have been by the sea, but that the ocean had receded in the course of centuries and the ruins lay well inland when he investigated them, covered by the sands of the desert. The old harbor was sanded over, sand dunes had smothered the sluices, and mighty dams lay buried beneath the veils of sand. The Bishop made every effort to push aside these veils. He dug and probed, and after a few years he had uncovered the ground plan of the city of Chan-Chan, which must have housed two hundred thousand inhabitants in its heyday.

The two chief buildings had double walls, and were thought to be palaces, but it is only in recent years that they have been examined thoroughly. The larger one had a perimeter of over half a mile. It contained its own reservoir and one wing was composed of peculiar cells arranged in five rows with nine chambers in each. The walls of these cells were of hewn stone and this was particularly striking because all the other parts, even the main walls, were built of mud bricks. At first it was suggested it must have been a prison block, but that did not fit in with the fact that there were steps leading to every cell as to an altar. When a Peruvian examined the smaller palace, he discovered it too had inner chambers of similar construction and these had not been completely stripped of their original contents. There were shreds of cloth and many ornaments made of shells; there were mummies and an idol of wood. This did not look like a prison either. Probably these cells with their walls of stone were temple chambers and it was here that the priests kept the sacred animals dedicated to the moon, the most revered of which was the snake. Chan-Chan means Snake City.

For the Chimus, who lived in a narrow strip of land between deserts, water was the life-giving element, and they thought of snakes as the waves of the desert. Snaky lines were the symbol for water, just as they were in the world of the Pharaohs. They were tirelessly repeated in woven patterns, on ornaments and walls, a device to unite the moon, the sea, and the rivers in complete harmony. These simple people saw the rivers as mighty snakes, bringers of life to the desert.

Chan-Chan was a rich town with gardens, terraces, and buildings whose walls were covered with a fine mortar and

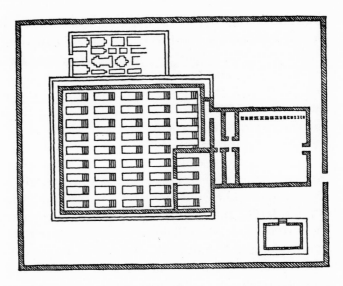

Plan of one of the "palaces" of the Chan-Chan

then adorned with stucco and lavishly decorated. The houses of the nobles were covered with beautiful roofs and had wooden verandas and curtains over the doorways. The town was divided into ten wards or districts in which the houses stood close together as in a fortress city. But there were also open squares and public gardens laid out according to a formal plan. The living quarters must have looked like a giant wasp's nest, for each clan had its own center, a honeycomb of activity which could easily be defended because it was surrounded by a high wall which enclosed it in an exact square. These wards were called after different animals, after the *huacas* sacred to the clans. Each community was self-contained behind its walls with its own temple, reservoir, and burial mound as well as dwelling houses and allotments.

Chan-Chan was not the only city by the sea. As the coastal tribes developed into settled communities there was nothing to do but to squeeze the houses closer together and share out land and water. Irrigation and water-conservation schemes were planned on a grand scale and canals, dams, and aqueducts were built, designed to hoard every drop of water for man and beast, and for cultivation. A network of canals was laid out right to the edge of the desert and it was true to say that hardly a drop of water was lost in the sea. Ditches were cut into the rock and where heights blocked the way, pipes were tunneled through the hills.

After a torrential cloudburst in the mountains, the rivers of Peru could rise so fast that the towns might well be flooded and washed out to sea. To reduce this danger, the Chimus built dams with sluice gates, and reservoirs to store the surplus water. The biggest of these was like a lake three-quarters of a mile long and it was held in by a dam whose base was eighty feet thick at the bottom. What remains of these dams and canals astonishes construction engineers who see them today. The biggest Chimu aqueduct was over sixty miles long.

To defend these vital arteries, the Chimus erected fortresses on the heights and built garrisons wherever the moun-

Chimu vessel in the shape of a house

tain passes could be used as gateways for invasion. The architects were clever in using every advantage which the terrain offered them, and although their masterpieces have fallen into ruin now, the first Spaniards saw them still intact.

In the midst of the great desert lay the fortress of Paramonga, not far from the river which the Indians called Huamán, "the falcon," and the Spaniards Rio de la Barranca, the river with the steep banks. In January 1535 Hernando Pizarro wanted to ford the river, but he and his twenty-five officers had great difficulty with their horses, and so they spent the night in the fortress. The builders had devised a multiple system of defense and if necessary, the grounds in front of the stronghold could be flooded with water. The hill on which the fortress stood rose one hundred and fifty feet above the valley and the building itself consisted of three tiers, the lowest of which was strengthened with bastions. The enemy had first, therefore, to climb the hill and scale the three stories. But even if by some lucky chance he succeeded in getting to the top, he had then to find a narrow entrance which led through a labyrinth of passages to a well-concealed portal. Unless he found this entrance he could not hope to capture the stronghold. Paramonga was about two miles from the sea and a second fortress stood opposite it on a rocky promontory three hundred and fifty feet high. This pair of citadels secured the southern gateway of the Chimu kingdom from any attack.

Hernando Pizarro and his companions stared in amazement at the paintings on the fortress walls, at the well-built gateway and the "Two Tigers" in front of the main entrance. Cieza de León, who saw Paramonga somewhat later, admired more than anything else its internal plumbing, for it had a built-in system of pipes which supplied even the top story with running water.

Only thirty years ago, Robert Shippee discovered the remains of a fortified wall the like of which had never been seen before in Peru. It was from the air that he saw it first, a wall which began in the bay of the Santa Valley, continued across the desert, and climbed uphill into the mountains. It was the great wall which used to enclose the Chimu kingdom. The tenth Inca tried for many years to storm it, but in vain, until he saw the light. Then he had a brainstorm, and cut off the water supply which was vital to the coastal kingdom.

But the mightiest of the Yunca buildings were neither their houses, fortresses, nor waterworks, but their pyramids. Flying south from Trujillo along the coastal strip which stretches for hundreds of miles, the air passenger can see several hundred mounds which were once pyramids. They were all built of mud bricks and rose in several tiers. In the largest of them all, twelve million of these adobe bricks, as they are called, were used. Near the mouth of the Jequetepeque were no less than seventy of these pyramids quite close together, and another thirty of them stood in and around Chan-Chan. In the Chira Valley one pyramid was almost three hundred feet wide and nearly four hundred feet long, and in the Casma Valley lies a shapeless mound which was the mightiest of them all three thousand years ago. But not a single pyramid has been left intact. All were robbed. Near what was once the town of Pacatnamu, there was one striking promotory which was known as the "*huaca* with two heads," because the saddle of the former pyramid had fallen in as a result of the reckless marauding of the treasure seekers.

Once these pyramids were of great beauty. Many of them had steep walls and most of them had a stairway on the northern side which led without a break to the highest platform, where the altar stood. As there were few natural heights along the coastal strip, the inhabitants built hills for themselves so that their holy places would tower above their houses. By raising their temples toward the sky, they believed they would enable the gods to look down on them

116

more easily. Near the pyramids the people built burial mounds so that the dead, too, would be strengthened and receive a share of heaven's blessings as they streamed down from the sky.

At the top of these pyramids the priests made sacrifices; blood was shed and gifts offered, especially gold and silver, for the Great Chimu demanded tribute in gold from the mountains. When the tenth Inca overthrew the Chimus, the golden spoils of war which the defeated had to bring to him in Cajamarca were not less than the treasure with which Atahualpa tried to buy his freedom from the Spaniards in that selfsame city.

During the course of four or five centuries, three small kingdoms arose on the coast out of the numerous petty valley communities, but not without war, as the pictures on their pottery show us. The biggest of them all was the kingdom of the Chimu, which stretched over six hundred miles from the equator to the Pativilca River. Even today there are the remains of a road which linked up all the most important places. Near Chan-Chan this road was eighty feet wide and it had walls to secure it against the encroachments of the sand dunes. It ran as far as the Nazca River, which shows that the three kingdoms must have been in communication with each other. Indeed, they were probably allies, and when the Chimu kingdom reached its highest stage of development they may even have been united. The Incas took over this road and extended it even further.

The heart of the Chimu kingdom consisted of three valleys, those of the Chicama, the Moche, and the Viru. Gradually more distant valleys were incorporated, until jungle, sea, and mountains were enclosed into a dominion which was larger than the whole of the empire of the eighth Inca.

The central part of the coast belonged to those tribes to whom the name of Cuismancu is given in the chronicles. The river valleys of the Chancay, the Ancón, and the Rimac

117

were all part of this smaller state. In the middle of it lay the shrines and the holy city where pilgrims came to worship the god of the sea, Pachacamac, the Great Speaker.

To the south was the state of Chincha. The Chincha tribes were warlike and they fought bitterly against Inca aggression. Here too there were pyramids and terraced buildings of squares of adobe brick. These bricks were so hard and enduring that even until comparatively recent times, people would pay up to ten times as much for them as for comparable modern building materials. But once the Sons of the Sun could dam the rivers, resistance to them meant almost certain death from thirst for the valley communities. So the little kingdoms were merged into the realm of the Incas, and the children of the Chimus, the Cuismancus, and the Chinchas were made to learn that it was the Incas alone who had built their towns and pyramids, who had constructed the dams, the roads, and the canals.

But secretly the old traditions remained alive and when the chroniclers asked the coastal Indians about their ancestors, stories cropped up on all sides about princes who had come with their followers from far across the sea.

Long, long before, it was said, a prince whose name was Naymlap had come to the Lambayeque Valley. He had arrived from the north with a flotilla of rafts, bringing with him his consort, his harem, many children, and a troop of warriors who were devoted to him. His court was composed of forty officers, such as the royal road-maker, the guardian of the throne, and the keeper of the jewels. There was a cupbearer and a cook, litter bearers and a herald, as well as an apothecary and a tailor who specialized in feather cloaks. Naymlap was said to have a particular weakness for such finery. The royal conch-blower was called Pita Zofi. When Naymlap walked along a path, servants had to strew it with the yellow dust of powdered shells. He must always have something of the sea beneath his feet, or he might lose his strength.

Naymlap and his court did not come with empty hands. The new arrivals brought wonderful textiles and objects with them that had never been made before in Peru. But their most precious possession was a green stone, a statue of the prince himself. This stone was placed in a temple which they erected not far from the sea, in the middle of the town, where they settled. Then they set to work and laid out fields and canals; and they prospered.

When Naymlap came to die, he took wings from the clouds and flew away. The people went to find him and in doing so they entered neighboring valleys and many remained there, "where they could hear the king's voice." So the kingdom expanded. Naymlap's son and heir was Cium. He had twelve sons who became the founders of great tribes. After a long rule, Cium felt that his end was approaching and he put himself into an eternal sleep. Ten further monarchs followed him. The last of them, Fempellec, a descendant of Naymlap, had the green stone statue moved to another place. The heavens were angry and took vengeance on him. Rain fell for thirty days and the fields were washed away into the sea. The people suffered great hunger and many of them died. Then the nation rose against Fempellec and threw him into the great floods.

Even in Pizarro's time, the memory of these kings was still alive along the whole of the coast, of princes who, like Naymlap, had come across the sea from the north, even as far as Chan-Chan, Rimac, and Nazca. These strangers brought many amazing things with them, and they built the first pyramids in Peru, in steps like those in Mexico and Yucatan.

The new land looked quite different from the homeland of these immigrants. They were dependent on the few rivers and on the sea. The rivers had brought green strips of life

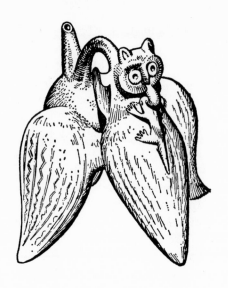

Mochica vessel

across the desert and the newcomers set about extending them. They scraped away the desert sand until they came to a layer of soil in which they could plant corn, potatoes, and many other things. The sea helped them to make enough grow. First the settlers learned to "plant little fishes"—that is, to use them as fertilizer. When they had settled down properly on the coast, they discovered that there was something even better for their crops than fish manure. That was guano, or bird droppings. With guano they increased the yield of their land thirtyfold. Now the few fields could support a much bigger population, and many hands were needed to build the pyramids, fortresses, and temples and all the towns which grew up in the era of the little kingdoms.

We know that six thousand Indians brought gold and silver from the mountains to the Great Chimu and that he had an army of weavers, potters, and goldsmiths to serve him and fill his palace and his kingdom with glory. But all the same the realm of the Chimu was shattered and the little kingdoms collapsed. Fortresses, towns, and pyramids turned to heaps of rubble. Dams, aqueducts, and canals fell in. The desert had its revenge. As soon as men began to fight and quarrel, it advanced with its crescent dunes over fields, gardens, and towns and turned the thousand-mile coastal strip into a paradise for archaeologists.

Excavators arrived from many different parts of the world. Some of them were Peruvians but the majority came from the United States, Germany, and France. For decades they have been searching for these remains of the world of the Yuncas which were partly buried when the Spaniards came. The Inca conquest changed many things, and even in their day the arts of the weavers, goldsmiths, and potters had lost their old greatness. Many of the workshops of the Chimus had become factories, engaged in the mass production of jars and dishes. The real crafts endured latest in the south, and it was the Chinchas who remained true to their own gods the longest, although in the central region the Great Speaker who had come out of the sea was worshipped still in Pizarro's time. All the villages within three hundred hours' traveling time brought offerings and sacrifices to Pachacamac's temple once a year.

Mochica painting

Ceremonial mace with the carving of a god at the top

On February 1, 1533, Hernando Pizarro rode down from Cajamarca to the coast, to the shrine of the Great Speaker. He and his men had come to rob the temple of its treasures. Priests barred their way, but Hernando trampled them down with his horses. The Spaniards rode through gateways and over broad flights of steps until they reached a courtyard in which there was a fountain. A fence of golden palings was woven around it, so that the fountain would always enjoy the bright gaze of the sun. Behind it was the sanctuary, a dark hole, in which was a wooden idol smeared with blood. The Spaniards brought it out into the light of day and there in the fountain courtyard they burned it to ashes. For the conquerors, Pachacamac was an idol whose oracle helped the priests to deceive their own and the Inca peoples. They rode on again in a hurry, more impressed with the temple than with the god. One of them wrote, "It seems doubtful if

Part of a manto (shroud). Paracas region

G. 3603.

such a building could possibly have been built without the help of demons."

Three hundred and fifty years later, archaeologists came to the same place, and they stood before the ruins, for the glory had departed. They had only rubble to work on shreds of cloth and splinters of pottery. But one of them was the great German scholar Max Uhle, and he was the first to start reading the history of Pachacamac from these fragments. He worked methodically and as he was also concerned with diggings going on at the same time both to the north and the south, he was the first to see the picture as a whole, in its true perspective. It is thanks to him that we know for a fact that the jars from the Moche Valley are older than was thought, that they are earlier than Inca pottery. No one could date vases which had been unearthed from the Nazca region, either, until Uhle brought a ray of light into the darkness.

Many other explorers followed him, notably Julio Tello, a Peruvian, who was the greatest discoverer of them all. On the rainless peninsula of Paracas, he found subterranean houses, storerooms, and rivers and a whole city of the dead, intact. Deep in the rock were domed chambers and square cells which contained hundreds of corpses wrapped in rich textiles. Some of the skulls had been raised or flattened surgically, and many had been trepanned, with the fractured bone replaced by sheet gold. There were nuggets of gold placed in the mouths and eyes of corpses too, and nowhere else in Peru were woven shrouds of such beauty ever discovered, although along the whole of the coast it was customary to provide lavishly for the dead and to give them generous funeral gifts.

In the Huaca de la Cruz, which had the reputation of being "a miserable handful" among treasure seekers, the

Gold mask with traces of red color. Ica style   123

American William Strong found a prince's grave. The body was wrapped in fine cotton and reed matting. Round about were jars, chests, feather fans, bottle gourds, and a scepter on which was carved a god accompanied by a boy.

The dead were always carefully equipped for their journey. Not long ago, a tomb was found on the northern coast and the priest buried there had been wrapped in a garment made of thirteen thousand gold sequins. He had been transformed into a golden fish so that he could dive into the sea of eternity.

In the hands of one old crone, so ancient that the gaps where her teeth had been were already closed, there were found three lumps of coloring matter, white, blue, and red, and by the side of the body there were the remains of a loom. There were flakes of copper sprinkled on her shoulders and a tiny piece of copper in her mouth.

These graves pose many riddles for us, and the pictures which the craftsmen wove and painted are not for us to understand. They point beyond this life to a more distant world. The Indians on the coast loved everything to do with the earth, but they considered heaven more important still. In the middle of the southern desert, for instance, there are mysterious lines and figures which have only been discovered since airplanes have been used for traveling. The sand of the desert there is dark and very stony, but the stones have been deliberately removed in certain places to pick out patterns and pictures on the ground, which make sense only if they can be seen from the air. There are white lines radiating from the hills in different directions as if they were searching for a particular spot. There are animals and cactus plants, all on a gigantic scale. There is a whale with a harpoon through it and a hummingbird with wings fifty yards long. Indeed, many of these pictures are hundreds of yards long, and the biggest actually measures five miles. It is only from the air that they can be seen and appreciated, yet they must surely have been carved out of the desert background to delight the gods, at a time long before airplanes were invented.

For many years explorers have been trying to explain these desert pictures, which are crusted over with the salty breath

Aerial view of lines and patterns carved in the ground near Nazca. On the right is the old Inca road, the dotted line marks the modern highway

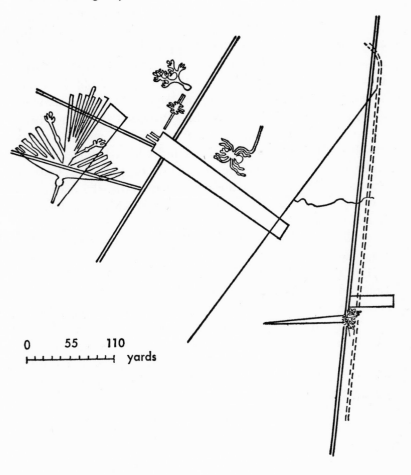

0   55   110 yards

of the sea. As many of them have Inca roads running across them, the pictures must have ceased to have any meaning by the time the Incas ruled, for they destroyed nothing that was sacred to the peoples whom they conquered. Many of the lines show up only when the sun rise. Are they some kind of calendar, perhaps? That they were meant to be seen from above is indisputable.

Research is still going on to find out more about the world of the Yuncas, and not only at the fringe of the desert and in the coastal valleys. On one of the islands off the coast which are covered with guano, archaeologists have been digging through layers of bird droppings. Recently they dug up a medallion with a coat of arms from Pizarro's day and in the deeper strata they found vessels from old Peruvian times. But the layers of guano can give only an approximate dating. The soil is more reliable. Provided it has not been tampered with, it can now be established with certainty which finds are from early times and which belong to more recent cultures. From the thousands of pots and textiles, masks and utensils, and the remains of walls, the excavators can put together a picture of the Yunca world. They look the inhabitants of the town of the dead straight in the face and they ask them, "Tell us how you lived, what you thought, and what you believed."

The lips of the mummies were often held together with thorns, but archaeologists are patient people. They ask until they get an answer. "Potter from the Moche Valley," they ask, "what are those pictures on your jars?" Or they will say, "Weaver woman from Paracas, what pattern is that on your shroud?" They turn to the mask maker from the central coast: "Tell us, mask maker, what lies hidden behind your masks?"

Secrets of
the Yunca world

This is what I say, I, the old potter from the Moche Valley:
My vases know more than I do. They have forgotten nothing.
They can tell you about the land of the Yuncas and every one
has a different story to tell, for I never made two alike. You
ask me why? Because no two trees are alike, no bird is the
same as another bird. No two stars in the sky are alike and
yet there are so many stars in the heavens that no one can
count them all. Pachacamac, the creator who emerged from
the sea, has made the Yunca earth in this way, so that nothing
is precisely the same as anything else. So how can we potters,
who are his tools, do otherwise? Whoever copies an article
so that it is exactly like another becomes an ally of Death the
leveler, who makes everything equal, and a copyist will lose
the power to create living things. That is the first rule which
the potter learns.

I learned my craft from my father. I watched him mold-
ing vases. He took in his hands a lump of clay in which there
was no life and in his hands it came to life. From a dead

127

lump there came a little house, a head, a gourd, or a musician, or just a plain jar. Then my father took colors and a brush, and suddenly there were fishes or foxes on the jar, dancing with one another, or there might be beans running a race around the vase. When the story was finished, the vase was fired and then it could never forget its story any more. For many years I learned by my father's side until I too could make jugs which lived, and from me my sons learned it too.

But now let my jugs speak; let them tell of the land of the Yuncas and its people just as it was in my day.

The land of the Yuncas lies by the sea between two deserts. The people live in the valleys where there are the rivers and the towns. The desert is all sand and wind with little life. But the sea is inexhaustible and it was from the sea that the creator god came forth. The hands of my father, my hands, the hands of my sons and grandsons are not enough to copy everything that the sea gives us: flounders, eels, and tuna and thousands of other fishes, rays and sharks which are dangerous and mysterious sea monsters which float like islands and have trees growing out of their backs. The Yunca people are fishermen and so they are familiar with the sea. They trail nets behind their rafts when they go out fishing and sometimes they use cormorants, the yellow-beaked ravens of the sea, to help them. This is how they do it. The cormorant perches on the edge of the raft, at the alert, and as soon as a shoal of fish swims by, it dives into the water. It is swifter than many kinds of fish, and in a moment it reappears with its prize, but it cannot swallow the catch itself for it has had a ring slipped around its neck that prevents it. So the fisherman removes the fish and the cormorant takes up its watch once more, and then it dives again and again until the man is satisfied and finally allows the bird to eat a fish for itself.

Many fisherman have a hard life. They carry their boats down to the sea on their shoulders, but these boats are light and easy to row for they are made of bundles of reeds. They

Mochica painting: A desert scene

carry fishing lines with copper hooks tied to them and the men go on fishing until the wind changes and sends them home again, riding over the surf. Among these fishermen are daring fellows who will tackle sharks and they always have harpoons lying ready at the bottom of the boat. Often seals come to the coast and then the fishermen turn hunter and surround the seals armed with clubs. They also hunt iguanas and this is not without its dangers, for the iguana bites when it is attacked. It is safer to catch lizards or snails. You spear them with a little pointed stick and then drop them in the basket over your arm. The Yuncas like a varied diet and they know what tastes good.

Mochica painting: A seal hunt

Big-game hunting is only for the aristocracy. They wear their best clothes for the hunt as if they were going to a festival. The ordinary people are only their beaters. First they spread out nets in the thick undergrowth and then the men and the dogs beat up the game. Andes deer and small stags are hunted with spears which are flung from a spear thrower, but other game is driven into the nets and clubbed to death. Only foxes are safe from the huntsman, for they stay awake at night and so are sacred to the moon. The only danger for the fox is from the dog, for it is a moon animal too. The moon is troubled when a dog chases a fox cub and the cub runs panting for its life, with its tongue hanging out of its mouth.

The rivers are hunting grounds too, and the Yuncas catch waterfowl and fish to eat. But the waterfowl are hunters on their own account. Here is a heron darting through the water like a gust of wind. The water lilies look on in horror as it snaps up its prey between the two long blades of its beak. The water is alive with fish and frogs, and no wonder, for the river comes from the sea. True, it is the rain which makes the rivers swell, but the rain comes from the clouds and they in their turn come from the big water.

This is the story the priests tell us: The creator god, who came out of the sea, led the Yunca people here and told them to build towns and temples, and dig canals so that the coastal valleys could expand and more could be grown in the fields —corn and manioc, spices, gourds and melons, cotton and agave. The sea blows away the breath of the desert. The sea gives little fishes and guano so that none of the Yunca people need go hungry, nor even the mice. There are grains of corn, peanuts, and even melons for them to eat.

So the potter shows a mouse nibbling at a nut, for the creator god made mice too. No living creature is too humble for the potter. There is nothing he ignores. That is the second rule he learns. He sees a tortoise sprawling on its

Mochica painting: Heron catching fish

back wriggling with its paws and head and trying to turn itself the right way up. He sees the gannet spreading its wings to protect its young, the deer suckling its fawn, sea lions romping in the sand, birds asleep, and the puma pouncing on the wayfarer. Whatever grows and moves here in this land finds a place on his wares. He observes what people do, how they live, and what they dream. Here is a young man plucking the down from his chin with tweezers and there a young woman washing her hair. The water is steaming hot and there is an agave blossom in it to make her hair as soft as the breeze. A child is sitting on the ground, searching for sand ticks between its toes.

Let me describe some of the other pictures which are painted on pottery: A man drags a pointed stick along the ground furrowing the soil. Another is making mud bricks. He leaves them out of doors in the gaze of the sun, which is good for them and makes them as hard as stone. Here the houses are built with open windows, an open door, and a light roof. There is no icy wind to fear and it seldom rains, so the only danger is from earthquakes. That is why the roof is always of straw, which will not hurt if it falls on your head.

There is little to fear from thieves either, for robbery is very rare. But if someone does steal, then the whole community rises against him. A stick with green leaves is set up in the street in which the theft took place and a search is made in every corner to find the culprit. Woe to him who hides a thief. He suffers the same fate as the guilty man. He is bound to a stake with a rope around his neck and a blind man holds the end. Hour by hour the rope is pulled tighter and tighter. For lesser crimes, the wrongdoer is beaten with sharp-edged stones. A high official found guilty of a crime is allowed to commit suicide so that the executioner's hand shall not touch him. The worst punishment is reserved for the man who sabotages canals and dams. His face is flayed while he is still alive, because he has endangered the lives of so many people.

The coastal people love life. They are devoted to their children, their houses, their fields, their animals, and their granaries. They are fond of trading and they undertake long journeys, even by sea. They weigh out their goods in prettily carved scales with nets hanging from the beam and their weights are pieces of copper or little bags filled with spices and corn. It is easy to tell by their fine clothes that merchants in the land of the Yuncas can make their fortune. Nor do the weavers, potters, or smiths go hungry. But even beggars have a place in this country. The coastal people love dancing, music, and noise. Entertainers and dancers travel far afield; there are musicians at all the feasts. With drums and trumpets, panpipes, rattles, and bells, the cares of everyday life are driven away. Even if most people wear rags, they enjoy themselves. Many of them pour so much *cabuya* juice down their throats that they cannot find their own way home. Two others steady the drunken man between them and show him the way.

The potter overlooks nothing. He sees how a child comes

Tumi *(ceremonial knife) with carved top showing trepanning (skull operation)*

into the world, how the mother washes the newborn baby and takes it to the doctor, who brews a drink from herbs. Another ventures to operate on a fractured skull although he knows what is at stake. If the operation does not succeed, the surgeon will be buried with the victim of his clumsiness, for he is considered the accomplice of death if his patient dies.

One jug tells what happens in war. A Mochica soldier has hit his enemy so hard with his club that the latter turns to flight. His chin is bleeding, there is horror in his eyes, and he drops his weapons to escape more easily. But the guardian angel of the Mochica warrior falls on him so that he cannot get away. Soon the fugitive will be taken prisoner and led by the rope like an animal, until his fate has been decided. He may be sentenced to carting bird dung from the guano islands, or he may bleed to death on the pyramid altar as a sacrifice to the gods. Then his blood will be offered to the sea eagle in a golden dish, as a gift to the sea and to the moon. The eagle takes the redness and carries it high above the sea into the sky. Then the moon gleams with a new glory and life begins again in the sea. Everything is commanded to increase and multiply and it is to this end that sacrifices are made, whether of human beings, of llamas, of fruits, or of golden vessels. The farmer plows, the weaver weaves, and the potter molds his jars, all to ensure the propagation of life.

And now I shall speak of the first potter. When Pachacamac had finished making the Moche River, he felt thirsty. So he made himself a jar and dipped it into the river to get water. Now there was life in the jar and because the creator had willed that the jar should live, he gave it a face. As he did so, he looked into the water and saw his own face. So they were his own features that the jar received. What he

Mochica painting: Warrior fleeing and throwing off his clothes

had made so pleased the creator that in his delight he created a Mochica man and gave him the jar for a head. That is why we potters of the Moche Valley make so many jars in the shape of human heads, those of princes and priests, of the powerful and wise, of the blind, the suffering, and the deformed, of those whose spirit is confused and those who have dangerous thoughts lurking behind their foreheads. In truth, it is Pachacamac who makes them all, just as he made the first one. But there are so many of them that he uses our hands for his work.

That is all I know, I, the old potter from the Moche Valley.

This is what I say, I, the old weaver woman from Paracas:
They gave me three colors when I went from the land of the Yuncas to the Land of the Dead, white, blue, and red, the colors of day, of night, and of life. This is what these colors mean on the cloth which we weaver women make, and every color must be in its right place, just as in speaking each word must be in its right place, so that the whole makes sense. If our colors were confused, what we wove would have no sense either. These pieces tell the story of the land in which I live now.

For seventy years long I wove cloth in the land of the Yuncas. First I watched my mother as she fastened one end of the loom to her girdle and the other to the edge of the roof, or tied it to a post which stood before the house. I watched her take a little bobbin and make it travel back and forth, in and out of the threads, and listened to her sing as she worked. She taught me the songs and she taught me how to weave. At first I made only small, simple pieces; then I tackled bigger ones until I could weave as well as my mother and make whole lengths which take a thousand days to complete.

These are winding sheets to shroud the dead so that evil

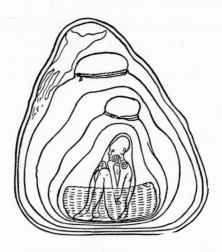

Mummy wrapped in cloth

demons cannot touch them while they are on the journey
to the Land of the Dead. For death has stunned them and
they need protection and rest so that they will recover their
senses and enter their new life. That is why fishes are woven
into these cloths, for fish bring life from the sea. That is why
birds are woven into them, for birds carry corn and seeds
from the fields. There are doors woven into the cloths, an
entrance and an exit. The dead man is wrapped in hundreds
of pictures surrounded by night swallows and hummingbirds
who tell him of the new year, by tadpoles and beans which
grow so quickly, by millipedes which never grow tired, by
good spirits to protect him from evil. These spirits have
cat's eyes to see in the dark, they have dog's tongues to harry
their enemies, they have human feet to find the path, they
have rafts to get to the Land of the Dead more quickly. Here
there is a great sea and the fishermen go out in boats which
are as alive as they are. The boats have two heads so that they
can speak to the wind and the water, and in these boats the
fishermen are carried to the temples which are alive too,

with snakes to support the roofs. Runners bring beans with them and the beans run races with the messengers. There are messages scratched on every bean, and the spirits play the bean game with them. The beans hop over dunes and cacti; they can glide through the air like birds, for even the desert is full of life in the Land of the Dead. And when a feast day comes, the spirits of the dead take rattles and trumpets; the dead sing their songs and wave sticks which have bunches of feathers tied to them and they dance a dance until the feather sticks turn into wings, until the dancers turn into birds and forget that they are dead. The shrouds slip away from them and they escape from the grave. The sky is open for them as it is for the birds; they can swing to the moon and play with the stars. Night for them is lighter than the day. Night is the day of the dead and there is no end to it.

The dead are given cloaks of feathers to take with them, so that they will be light enough to swoop to the sky. It takes thousands of feathers to make such a cloak, hummingbirds' feathers which are so tiny that twenty of them are needed to cover a fingernail, feathers from the green-headed *camantiva*, whose wings are blue with shining red dots, yellow *chayna* feathers and white *tandia* feathers, hundreds of wingbeats to carry the dead through the Land of the Dead, where even black feathers have a glossy gleam. The Land of the Dead is a land of joy, and it stands open for everyone except one, except for Death. Death who goes limping through the land for many years before he can catch a human being, he alone may not enter the Land of the Dead.

The dead man lives in a sea which is deeper than any sea. He lives in a desert brimming over with life. The cacti put forth golden snakes, the stars are like flowers which never fade, foxes streak like crescent moons over the sand dunes, and fishes play in and out of the dunes as they do among the waves. There is no shortage of water. The Rain God beckons

137

Mochica painting: Spirits of the dead with rattles and flutes

to his boys and they fetch their jugs and set them out and the spirits of the wind romp through the clouds. Then the Rain God puts on his cap of clouds, and the heavenly funnel between his eyes fills with rain and all the jugs are filled to overflowing.

These are the pictures on the great shroud in which I am wrapped. It is the cloth which Pachacamac himself wove when he came out of the sea. That was on the first day and

Mochica painting: Warrior being transformed into a bird

Part of a human face. A pottery fragment found in Tiahuanaco

this is what happened. Pachacamac wiped the water from his eyes and looked up and the darkness over his head was so deep that he was afraid. So he wove the stars into the sky and he covered up all the darkness, and thus he became the first weaver. He made the cloth which wraps all life in it, but for all other lengths of cloth he uses our hands. He himself has woven a tapestry in which no picture is forgotten and the white, the blue, and the red are all one.

That is all I know, I, the old weaver woman from Paracas.

This is what I say, I, the mask maker from the central coast:
I will speak of the one who breathes behind all the masks, of the Great Speaker. What I know of him I know from the priests through whom he speaks.

They say that there was another god before Pachacamac. He was called Kon and he was formless, like a cloud, taking any shape he chose. He created good land by the sea and he made his people very beautiful, so that when these men rose against him, Kon was overwhelmed with rage. So first he sent a flood which drowned all the people and then he made it so that it would never rain in this land again, and the coastal strip became a desert. Then Pachacamac emerged from the sea and drove out Kon who, in his wrath, had forgotten that a god must be merciful. Pachacamac caused rivers to flow down from the mountains into the desert and he brought men down from the sky. Three eggs as big as stars fell to earth, one of gold, one of silver, and one of copper, and from them emerged all the Yunca nation, the kings, the princes, and the people. Pachacamac saw that his creatures were hungry, so he fished up from the sea all that was left of the people whom Kon had created. Pachacamac sowed their teeth and corn grew; he planted their bones and they became manioc bushes and potatoes; he sowed heads and they

(Above) "The Gateway of the Sun" at Tiahuanaco
(Below) Looking across Lake Titicaca

grew into pumpkins. Now it was possible for the people to live along the coast. For every man the god created an invisible brother who went with him to see that he did not lose his way. But as all mankind was created from the stars, there is a shining light within them which is called *illa*. And when a man returns to the stars, the light breaks from him and then it can be seen. So it is with my masks. Molten gold is poured into the mold, but it is only when the mold is broken that my mask shines forth.

When I was still a mask maker, I lived in the town near Pachacamac's temple which stands in the middle of the land. I often went into the temple with the pilgrims who came there. They brought their questions and laid them before the god, and when the Great Speaker answered them, then the masks which the priests wore shone with a great glory. And the faces of those pilgrims gleamed too as if a light was shining within them. But all the light came from the Great Speaker: the priests knew that.

Pachacamac is a god who has mercy on mankind. He is a god of peace, not a god of wrath. The pilgrims on the way

Chimu pottery

to his temple must not carry weapons. They travel unmolested even through hostile territory. The Great Speaker puts out the fire that threatens the land and its cities, that is, the threat of war. He tempers the gaze of the sun so that the whole land does not become a desert. He is the keeper of the earth and he answers mankind. When they came to him for the first time and asked him how they should live, then his joy was great. On his face appeared a glory which turned into pure gold, into the first mask. Instead of an answer, the god of the oracle gave his face to mankind. So he was the first mask maker. That is all I know, I, the mask maker from the central coast.

The kingdom of the giants

Pilgrims came even from the highlands of Peru to the shrine of Pachacamac, the creator of the Yunca world. They came down to the Rimac Valley to consult the Great Speaker. The routes through all these coastal valleys were older than the Inca roads, and along them came the llamas carrying gifts for the gods or goods for trading, and now and then hordes of warriors on the warpath. These roads linked the sea with the *puna* and the adobe pyramids with the granite cities. But no one can say in which direction they were first built and no one knows for certain which towns are the older.

Up in the mountains there are ancient ruins and among them lie blocks of stone with razor-sharp edges and surfaces as smooth as glass. They weigh many tons, and when one sees them for the first time they immediately suggest giants. And there are giants there too, stone colossi up to twenty-two feet high, covered with mysterious runes. There are gateways as well, enormous portals hewn out of a single block of stone. And yet the openings are not big enough for a giant to pass through. Even a man of average height would have difficulty in using them. One of these gates, the Puma Punku, or Lion's Gate, has an opening measuring only two feet by sixteen inches. Was it a gate for lions, for the god who, in the world of stone, took the form of the puma?

The stone portals, the statues, and the blocks stand in a wilderness where no trees or shrubs grow, a desolation wholly exposed to the winds which blow down from the glaciers. There are cracks and fissures and caves in these rocks and from the depths comes the rumble of thunder. This is a world still in a state of becoming. It is the world of the condor, a naked world high above the desert valleys and the jungle. It lies hemmed in by the mountain peaks, lifeless and ashen. But the moment the sun rises, its hidden beauty is revealed. Colors come bursting out of the gray and in notes of red, blue, yellow, and black, the *puna* sings its hymn to the morning: "I am alive!" is the song it sings.

Up here, 12,500 feet above sea level, the country of Peru has its eye wide open to the sky, the Lake of Titicaca. This great eye gives life to the wilderness. It brings the sky down to earth and fetches the icy peaks from the horizon. A stairway of silver steps mirrors itself in the lake, and it was up these steps on the first day of the creation that the sun and the moon mounted to the firmament. The creator made them both on the two big islands in the lake, so the legend goes.

The lake feeds the men who live on its banks, it gives them fish and birds and the reeds from which they make their boats, their sails, and the roofs of their huts. In barely accessible hiding places, on floating islands of reeds, there still live today the Urus who were there in the beginning, and it is easier to lure a pike from its hiding hole beneath the bank than to entice an Uru from the secret habitation where he fishes and lives.

Today the lake is one hundred and ten miles long. Once

it was larger still, and even in the days when the fourth Inca ruled, its waves beat against the steps of a stairway which led to the temples with the stone giants. But even the first Inca saw the temple only as a ruin. The other temples too, as well as the bases of the pyramids which rise on the southern bank of the lake, were already destroyed when Mayta Capac found them.

Who built them? The tribes who lived there told what they knew. They spoke of "the time of darkness before there was the sun."

The town is called Tiahuanaco, but the name is as puzzling as the statues and the gateways, and how old it is no one can say.

Tiahuanaco! "Guanaco Place," "Deriving from the Crea-

144

tor," "God of Lights," "Stone in the Middle": these are only four interpretations among many. It cannot even be proved conclusively which language the word belongs to: Aymará, Colla, or Quechua.

The Incas laid their hands on Tiahuanaco as well. When they came to power they declared that they were the founders of the mysterious city. The "rethinkers" in Cuzco invented a derivation which would add to the fame of the fourth Inca, Mayta Capac. This is what they said: "Mayta Capac was standing on the southern bank of Lake Titicaca one day when he received an important message. The courier had run so hard that he collapsed when he had delivered it and the Inca praised his swiftness and told him, 'Tiay Huanaco! Rest now, Guanaco!' And he ordered a city to be built on the spot to commemorate the event." This is but one of the legends which went to build up the great Inca deception, that before they reigned there was no civilization.

The tribes around the lake did not dare to contradict them nor, indeed, to think anything different right up to the time of the last Inca. It was only when the Spaniards came to Tiahuanaco "to fetch big golden nails and many kinds of golden vessels" that the spell was broken. But by then, the inhabitants could neither say nor confirm who had founded the town. And even today the question remains unanswered although scholars have been asking it for centuries.

One man who lived in La Paz, the capital of Bolivia, which is not far away, devoted his whole life to solving the riddle. He was Arthur Posnansky. By profession, he was not an archaeologist at all but a civil engineer who owned a large brickworks. When he came to Tiahuanaco for the first time, he saw the dark huts and the gables with horns or crosses on them. He saw the great blocks of stone which were built into the brick walls of the church, and he wondered where they had come from. Soon he found out. There was a field of rubble some distance away in an isolated spot, abandoned even by the lake, which had receded some twelve miles to the north. All kinds of ruins were lying there: flights of steps, upright or overturned, gateways, stone colossi, and megaliths, and all in such confusion that it looked as if a city had suddenly been destroyed without warning, perhaps by a deluge or a volcanic eruption. But there were no traces of either lava, mud, or ashes, and no signs of any earthquake violent enough to have shattered the pyramids or the walls which were made of blocks weighing many tons each.

Posnansky measured these blocks and calculated how heavy they were. Not a few of them weighed as much as thirty to fifty tons apiece, and they must have weighed roughly twice as much before they were hewn into shape. They were so skillfully worked that they gave the impression they had been cast in metal. Posnansky looked for the nearest quarry and found that it was three miles away. What kind of people were they who had shifted great rocks from place to place as if they had been no more than the sunbaked bricks used on the coast? Were they giants? Even today, the natives call one of the huge stone statues discovered "The Giant" and another one "Big Brother."

Posnansky began to dig. He too found gold nails and utensils as well as fragments of pottery, vessels, and masks. He discovered graves, but their occupants, far from being giants, were rather shorter than he was himself. There were subterranean houses too and no one could stand upright inside them. There was hardly room for a man to squat, chin on knee. Posnansky, who had had much to do with the highland Indians and was familiar with their way of living, had often seen a man crouching in a corner like that, fallen fast asleep.

Posnansky dug and researched for many years, and what he found he carried off to a museum which he had had built himself, paying the workmen he employed out of his own pocket. He dug and collected with desperate haste, for others

146

besides himself were interested in these remains. Building firms saw in Tiahuanaco the ideal quarry with stone ready cut, an excellent source of cheap raw materials. Whatever was too heavy to remove they demolished with explosives, and dynamite was used to break up the megaliths and blocks and even the statuary. Posnansky wrote indignant letters to the newspapers and forced his way into various ministries, but the vandalism did not stop. On the contrary. Now "excavators" came armed with full authority from these same ministries, and if anything, they behaved worse than the commercial concerns. They even removed exhibits from Posnansky's own museum.

Posnansky photographed everything he found as quickly as possible, but the moment his back was turned, he could hear explosions going off and the destruction continued. So he had carried off to safety whatever he could. Even the giants were removed and the walls of Tiahuanaco with their huge blocks and columns were rebuilt in La Paz. Now the experts protested. Posnansky was falsifying the picture, they clamored. He should have left everything where it belonged. And this they said of a man who had seen for many years exactly what happened when you left things where they belonged! Tiahuanaco had developed into such a free-for-all that Posnansky did the only thing which remained open to him: tried to move faster than the others and salvage what he could. But in the eyes of many people, he was a fool who deluded himself into thinking that if only he went on asking questions long enough, the stones would yield and give him an answer. Posnansky never stopped asking and he never stopped dreaming either, until he found an answer.

This was what the stones told him, the obstinate dreamer, who would not leave them alone.

Tiahuanaco was not built "in a day" as it says in the legend. It took centuries. There were five quite distinctive periods in which building took place and the oldest of them dates from the primitive people who used to crouch in their subterranean huts at night, as in caves. They used greywacke and sandstone to make double walls and to sculpture the great stone figures which were their gods. Then one day, the lake grew wild and rough and a flood rose which destroyed the half-finished town.

The second period was that of immigrant Colla tribes, who settled there and whose descendants still live in the vicinity today. Among them were builders and smiths the like of which have never been seen since. They built the temples out of these huge blocks and they used copper cramps to hold them together. But this epoch, too, ended in catastrophe. Others came and finished their work. The newcomers built granite pillars into the walls, and, as in Machu Picchu or the palace of the Inca Roca, polygonal stones were used in construction. The fourth period was that of adobe brick building and the fifth was that of the Incas.

Posnansky had no doubt at all that he had interpreted the stones aright. One gateway especially aroused his curiosity. It had a frieze running around it on which numerous figures were carved, and finally Posnansky came to the conclusion that it was a "calendar stone." He discovered too that all the temples were built to face certain constellations, and allowing for the slight deviation which, according to Posnansky's views, had occurred since it was erected, he calculated that

"Stone seats" of Tiahuanaco

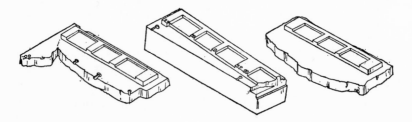

the gateway must be sixteen thousand years old. To crown it all, he wrested an extraordinary secret from the ruins, and this was it: That the whole of the highland plateau of Peru, including Lake Titicaca, had risen many thousands of feet since building was first started in Tiahuanaco and so—this was Posnansky's last word—this must have been Paradise, the Garden of Eden. It was here that mankind originated; this was the oldest city in the world: Tiahuanaco.

It was not only the archaeologists who shook their heads at such startling revelations in the book which Posnansky wrote about his findings. His theories did not hold water at all, yet only a man wholly obsessed by his task could have saved so much for posterity singlehanded. What he rescued from destruction is priceless and his services to history greatly outweigh his farfetched theories.

Archaeologists have been working now for several decades in Tiahuanaco, investigating a field which is, at last, strictly preserved. No more explosions shatter the silence. Indeed, even accredited research workers are hardly allowed there today unless they are Bolivians, and it has been difficult to get a permit to excavate for the last thirty years. When Wendell Bennett applied in 1932, he was only allowed to work on ten sites, but at the very first digging, he unearthed the twenty-two-foot-high stone figure which the Indians call "Big Brother." By now, deeper strata still have been uncovered, and Posnansky's first theories have been corrected and amplified. With every year we can see more clearly how Tiahuanaco once looked and imagine the buildings that stood there thousands of years ago.

The center of the town was a level clearing covering roughly one-sixth of a square mile. Here were the main buildings, and four of them were of exceptional size. The biggest of all was the Acapana, a terraced pyramid nearly fifty feet high, whose base was constructed of a mixture of pebbles and earth and faced all around with stone. Each side

149

was about 690 feet long. Built into the base was a kind of reservoir with an overflow canal which led into the open. Except for a few ruins, the walls which crowned the base have disappeared.

Of the second building, the Calasasaya, there remain only some square blocks and a row of "standing stones" or monoliths. Many of them are carved with symbols. The building measured approximately 445 by 425 feet. Inside it was a sunken courtyard and this was reached by a staircase whose individual steps weighed several tons each. In the northwestern corner stands "The Gateway of the Sun," Posnansky's "calendar stone."

Somewhat apart from these two principal buildings is the "Palace of the Coffins," as the Spaniards named it. All that remains of it now is a quantity of beautifully hewn masonry.

The fourth mighty ruin includes the Puma Punku, the Lion's Gate. It is also called the "Ten Gateways" or "The Water Gate." On this site there are portals, stone seats, and altars, staircases, and statues with turbans around their heads. Some are completed and others are only half finished. The confusion is so great that it seems as if life once came to an abrupt stop. What great catastrophe interrupted these craftsmen at their work will probably never be established in spite of all our finds, but the archaeologists have learned much from these figures of basalt, greywacke, and red sandstone in whose deep eye sockets there once flashed gold and precious stones. They have learned much too from the slabs of trachyte and andesite and from the megaliths, but their interpretations often contradict each other. What for one was a fortress with living quarters and granaries, workshops, and reservoirs was for another "The greatest Temple of the Sun on this earth." Posnansky confirmed that the Puma Punku with its double walls and ten gateways had been built on a base rising in four tiers. All the biggest buildings were built on pyramid foundations, and in all of them there

150

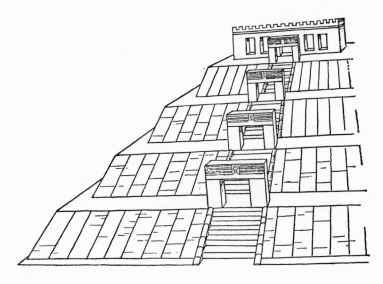

Reconstruction of a temple pyramid (Puma Punku)

were sunken chambers with stone walls. Many blocks are carved with a stone face. Some scholars considered that these chambers were used for reservoirs and that the passages which led from them were air ducts. But these air ducts are six feet high and the chambers contain not only stone faces but doorways, and there are signs that they housed something once. Altars? Thrones? Or coffins? Were there secret tombs in these pyramids as there were in Egypt? Were the stone cells sunken rooms for the ruler, or for the god to whom the shrine was dedicated? Were these chambers the homes of the sacred jaguars as the temples near the coast housed sacred snakes?

The image of the jaguar is found time and again in Tiahuanaco and it is a jaguar's face which dominates the most impressive of all the gateways, the Inti Punku. This is cut out of a single block of andesite nearly thirteen feet wide and ten feet high. Obviously it does not stand on the

151

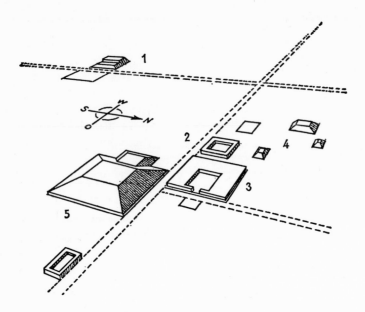

Plan of Tiahuanaco: 1. Puma Punku 2. "Palace of the Coffins"
3. Calasasaya with the "Gateway of the Sun" 4. Small pyramids
5. Acapana

spot for which it was originally intended and there is a big
crack in the stonework. The frieze which runs right around
it was never finished. This "Gateway of the Sun," which was
broken and askew, was restored in 1918 and since then it
has stood on the site where it was re-erected.

Forty-eight different kinds of winged creatures can be
made out on it, all carrying condor-headed scepters as they
hurry toward the central figure. This is unmistakably a
supreme god, one who rules over everything, and it com-
bines the features of a human being and a jaguar, a condor,
and a snake. Jaguar heads break out around its countenance
like the sun's rays and beneath the enormous eye sockets
where little suns were once embedded there are traces of

tears. The god weeps life, as did the sun according to the old legends of the highland tribes.

On another gate there are fishes instead of birds, and these are dedicated to the moon, as well as snakes which belong to the earth. Which was the supreme god for the builders of Tiahuanaco?

Ancient myths which have endured longer than the Inca lies tell of immigrants who came from far away and built their temples to face the stars. Earlier still, bearded figures made their appearance. But the beginning of all life in the highlands, so the chroniclers learned, was made by a god called Viracocha, the creator with the jaguar head who weeps golden tears. Viracocha created the first men from stone and they were giants. When these stone men rose against him he destroyed them and created men as we know them now. But he gave them the strength of giants all the

Central figure from the "Gateway of the Sun"

same and they had special powers over rock and stone. Amauta was the name which they gave their kings, and they founded the kingdom of Pirua. There they reigned for many hundreds of years, and their sacred city was Tiahuanaco.

A Spanish historian, the Jesuit Fernando Montesinos, made a list of one hundred and two Amautas, each of whom had reigned for about thirty years in the Kingdom of the Giants. The first ruler was called Pirua Manco and the kingdom of Pirua was called after him. According to Montesinos it was in the year 1220 B.C. that the Amauta Pirua Manco took over his kingdom.

Who was this Montesinos who wrote so confidently about Pirua and where did he get his information?

Montesinos came to Peru in the year 1628. There he remained for fifteen years, baptizing the Indians, inspecting mines, and traveling widely through the countryside. When he returned to Spain, he wrote a book so full of improbable tales that scholars have dubbed him the Munchausen of Peru. Indeed, many historians considered it a thick pack of lies from beginning to end, and it is quite true that many of the statements which Montesinos makes are pure invention. According to him, for instance, the first Peruvian was Ophir, a descendant of Noah!

But what Montesinos wrote about the hundred Amauta kings was not pure invention. He got that from a book written by a certain Blas Valera. And Blas Valera is a much more reliable source than Montesinos. Like the "Inca" Garcilaso de la Vega, he had Indian blood in his veins. Like Garcilaso, he was born in 1540, the son of a Spaniard who had come to Peru with Pizarro, and an Indian princess. Blas Valera grew up in Cajamarca, the town where Atahualpa was executed. At the age of twenty-eight, he became a Jesuit in Lima, and for the next twenty-three years he remained in Peru, travel-

River scenery. Northeast Peru

Sandstone sculpture of Tiahuanaco

ing widely and baptizing Indians. He worked at several missions in Peru, and then he visited Spain in 1591. He was in Cádiz when the English sacked the town, and two of the three books he had written were lost in the ruins.

Blas Valera was a chronicler who did not rely on the books of others. He was born in Peru and he lived there for fifty-one years. His Indian blood, his knowledge of several Indian languages, a careful education, and much travel helped him to explore the history of worlds which had disappeared long before and to root out legends and traditions which remained concealed from others who were not so well equipped. The book that survived the destruction of Cádiz was brought to La Paz in 1604. There Montesinos saw it in a

Jesuit school. He read what Blas Valera had written about Pirua and the Amautas, and the list of kings so inspired Montesinos that he "traced" Peruvian history all the way back to Ophir, the descendant of Noah. It was three hundred and forty years after Noah's flood, wrote Montesinos, that Ophir discovered Peru.

As the list of Amauta kings does not occur in any other chronicle, it has been doubted rather than studied, but some leading historians take it seriously. The North American scholar Philip Ainsworth Means places the kingdom of Pirua in the millennium between A.D. 200 and 1200. Pirua, the founder of the first dynasty, was no "idol worshipper," as Montesinos puts it, but a king who knew that there was only one god in heaven and earth, the creator to whom he gave the name Illaticci Viracocha.

It was during the reign of the thirteenth Amauta that there happened certain events which had profound consequences for Peru. This is what the chronicle has to say:

The thirteenth Amauta was a good ruler, so that his land had peace. Then the prophets and the sacrificial priests told him that a great turn in events was at hand. The Amauta grew very frightened at this prophecy. After a few days, there came messengers from the coast with the news that a great horde of strangers had landed there. They had come on rafts from the north and were invading the coastal valleys. At their head strode a powerful man, taller than all the others, although they too were giants. Then the Amauta sent out his spies to find out what kind of people they were, what weapons they carried and how they lived. The spies came back and reported: "Wherever these giants have penetrated, the only safety is in flight. The whole of the coastal strip has fallen into their hands."

Then the ruler of the highlands had all the fortresses strengthened. But the invaders never tried to overpower the Amauta kingdom. The danger came from the south instead.

About A.D. 450, warlike tribes attacked Pirua. The Amauta, who led the defense and tried to ward off this attack, died. His successor was attacked from the rear by the coastal dwellers. So the tribes from the south managed to establish themselves in Pirua and set up their gods in the temples. Fate could not be resisted any more. The kingdom of Pirua collapsed about A.D. 500 and Tiahuanaco was sacked for the first time.

It was built anew. With greater glory than ever before, the Amauta kings rebuilt their kingdom and Viracocha entered an even more beautiful temple. The kingdom by the coast flourished too, but Pachacamac was at peace with Viracocha. The heavens were watched by astrologers in the highlands as well as on the seashore. Gnomon pillars were erected to observe the sun's meridian altitude and the calendar was improved more and more. It was said of one of the Amautas that, in all the decades of his reign, he never laughed, because he learned so much from the stars, more than the astrologers and wise men. He constructed many sundials.

It was about A.D. 725 that the people from the south attacked the Pirua kingdom for the second time. The Amauta's army had to defend their country along mountain passes which were threatened by avalanches, but twice the aggressors were pushed back. Then other tribes from the east, themselves in flight and searching for more fertile soil, pressed forward to Pirua. The Amauta was master of the twofold danger and the kingdom was saved. But several centuries later, when Titu Pachacuti was on the Amauta throne and his realm was similarly threatened, he did nothing at all, but left everything in the hands of the gods. He made sacrifices daily as the priests counseled him, but it was only when the enemy had already entered the heart of the land that he led an army against them. There was a battle at Pucara, west of Lake Titicaca, and the Amauta army was defeated. Titu was killed and his surviving soldiers fled, carrying the body of

157

their king back to the town that was never occupied by invaders from the south. The defeat was followed by risings in the provinces and the kingdom of Pirua broke up. In a secret palace a child was placed on the Amauta throne, but Tiahuanaco was destroyed for the second time. That is what Montesinos wrote, basing his story on the account given by Blas Valera.

Modern excavations have proved conclusively that Tiahuanaco was in fact destroyed many times, but they do not reveal if the destruction was caused by hostile tribes or if there were violent revolutions when rival dynasties contended for the rulership. We know from another continent that it does not need attacks from without to overthrow a regime of builders of pyramids. The Old Kingdom of the Egyptian Pharaohs was destroyed from within because the people of the Nile began to doubt if the Pharaohs were the Sons of the Sun. The Pharaoh Unas had ancient texts carved into the walls of the burial chamber in the pyramid he had erected to be his eternal palace. These were considered magic formulas which would assure his ascent to the gods when he died. But unauthorized eyes read them and the mysteries were unveiled. What was believed to be the key to eternity, which had hitherto been entrusted only to the Pharaohs, fell into other hands; and now that the people were in possession of the "word of God," they rose against a ruler who had not been strong enough to keep the secret to himself. In the report of the destruction of the Old Kingdom, it was written: "The secret of the pyramids has been betrayed. The palace has been turned upside down overnight." In Tiahuanaco, too, excavation has shown that the temple walls, the stairways, and the megaliths were "turned upside down" in just the same way. The blocks of the Puma Punku look very much as if life had ceased "overnight."

What remains of the city shows that the Amautas were rulers capable of great achievements. They were builders of

Bowl of the Tiahuanaco period

pyramids, cities, and temples. They were kings of great wisdom, who taught the peoples they had united in their kingdom. Their realm was large and it spread almost to the coast and as far as the jungle.

In the days of the Incas, *amauta* was the name which was given to the monarch's counselors, the "wise men." And for the whole of Peru, the Amauta god Viracocha became the creator. An Indian chronicler has quoted a prayer of the fifth Inca's in which it says, "Oh come, Viracocha, ruler of all the world, great as the heavens, source of all things, creator of mankind. I greet thee ten times over. Thee do I seek with my eyes turned to the ground as I seek a spring when I am thirsty. With all the voice I possess, I call on thee."

Another prayer contains these words: "The eternal lord,

159

symbol of the world, the everlasting source. He gives the sign for all life. He makes our thoughts. He is the sun of suns, the creator of this earth, Viracocha."

According to the old beliefs of the Aymará and Colla tribes, before the day of the creation the world was a thick morass which lay in darkness. These were the times of Tutayac-Pacha, the long night. The first words which Viracocha spoke were, "Gather together," and this he said to the waters and then there were lakes and seas and dry land. But everything was still in darkness and there was no life on the earth. Then Viracocha breathed upon the earth and only then, when his spirit was upon them, could plants and animals and even men have life. Then for the second time, Viracocha said, "Gather yourself together." This time he said it to the darkness. And the darkness went within itself and drew out the light. So were created day and night, the light and the dark. Only then did the creator god make the sun and moon to light up the daytime and the night.

Viracocha means earthmaker and creator of mankind. The first men whom he had created made him angry, so he had them drowned in a great flood. When the waters had gone down for the second time, Viracocha called new tribes to life, above all those in the region of Lake Titicaca. He made only one man and one woman of each tribe, and he painted on their bodies the clothes they should wear. To some he gave long hair and to others short hair. He gave them the languages they should speak, the songs they should sing, and he put in their hands the seeds for sowing. He did not make these new men from stone but out of clay and when he had finished them all he breathed life into them as he had breathed it into the earth. Then he spoke: "Go down into the earth and each one shall emerge from where I tell him." Some of them came out of trees and some from springs or caves, and each tribe began to increase and spread. But the place of origin remained sacred to each tribe and it was

160

there that the founder of the tribe was turned into a condor or a bear or a stone when he died. Viracocha gave each tribe a different *huaca* so that they should be able to distinguish one from the other.

Among one of the highland tribes, the Cañari, the story of the great flood has been handed down in a slightly different form. They say that it hurt Viracocha to destroy mankind, but since a god can do nothing against his own wishes, he could not warn the rebellious sinners. So he told the llamas of a certain shepherd what was about to happen, and these llamas drove the shepherd and his wife to the top of a high mountain and there they and the llamas survived the flood.

One recurring theme in all these Viracocha myths is that this god was deeply concerned for mankind. He fashioned them twice, first of stone and then of clay, first as giants and later as he was himself, in his own image.

In the *puna* around Lake Titicaca there are strange towers with images of Viracocha carved in their walls. These towers are called *chullpas* and in them the dead were laid. The Indians told the first Spaniards who came to the district of Qutimbo that these charnel houses had been erected in unimaginably distant times, "even before the sun." The Spaniards were amazed at such stupidity on the part of these Indians. Before the sun? That could never be.

But it could, even if not as the Spanish conquerors interpreted it, for they did not listen to the Indians with a sympathetic ear. "Before the sun" meant at a time in which the sun was not for them the most important of the heavenly bodies. For even in the mountains, the moon was worshipped "before the sun." That can be read plainly in the images and the carved stones of Tiahuanaco. Not only are the signs for the sun engraved there but those for the moon and the earth as well. Viracocha, the creator god, has a jaguar head, and the jaguar was sacred to the moon, as were the fish and the snakes represented a hundred times over in the gateways of Tia-

Painted goblet. Coastal Tiahuanaco

huanaco. The surprising thing, though, is that there are
spreading rays around the puma's head, like the typical image of the rising sun. Winged creatures bring a message to
Viracocha, condor heads appear on the scepter which he
holds. The figures which serve him carry coronets of light,
like the mountains at dawn of day. The sun comes to the
moon, is the message which is conveyed on the great gateway
of Tiahuanaco. Moon and sun are devoted to the earth: that
is the meaning of the jaguars and condors surrounded by
snakes. Day and night are reconciled; to the gleam of silver
is added the glint of gold. The moon weeps the tears of the
sun so that the earth may blossom.

The region around Lake Titicaca, which is now grassland,
must have looked quite different in those days. In order to
build the pyramids and the great temples, it needed an army
of craftsmen, and in order to sustain such an army, it needed
a wealth of cultivated land. True, the legends of the Pirua
kingdom say that the blocks of stone moved of their own
accord when the Amautas beckoned to them, that they moved
to the sound of horns and even found for themselves the
places which the architects had designated for them. But this
was, so to speak, an effort to present the power and the wisdom of the Pirua kings in the best possible light. It is doubt-

ful if the builders of Tiahuanaco looked like giants, but giants they were for all that, mighty men for whom nothing was impossible.

Not only did they build this unique temple city on the southern shore of the lake. They laid out many towns in the highlands and made provision for sufficient food to be cultivated in the *puna*. In the country bordering on Cuzco, an archaeologist, John Rowe, found remains of stone walls which were older than any Inca buildings. Wendell Bennett discovered double walls in Chiripa and stone pails with highland corn in them. Many explorers take the view that Tiahuanaco was a city of shrines, a holy city built by the hordes of pilgrims who assembled there in the course of centuries. Certainly Tiahuanaco was a city of temples. But the builders did not need to come from far away in the first place. They lived by the lake. Stone pipes carried drinking water down from the mountains. Sketches of buildings on slabs of stone show that plans were drawn in advance and near each temple there was a workshop of considerable dimensions. Broad white strips of stuccoed paving are evidence that Tiahuanaco must have been a splendid city once.

Whoever built a town like that could also build a kingdom. The finds and researches going on at the present day show more and more clearly that the builders of Tiahuanaco were men of outstanding ability. Their god who joined the moon and the sun became the most exalted of the Inca gods and he was only dethroned with the arrival of those bearded men whom the Indians believe were his sons; for when this god left Peru, he promised that he would come back one day.

The image of Viracocha penetrated into the coastal valleys too. His features can be traced in feather cloaks and on pottery, although he looks a milder, kinder god than he is in the highlands. But still he is unmistakable, holding in his hands the scepter with the condor heads, with bird's wings—or corn. The god of tears gave his face to the coastal people too

163

and they worshipped him for hundreds of years. Textiles and pottery took forms which had originally appeared in stone in Tiahuanaco. Just as the rays break forth from the jaguar's head on the mighty Gateway of the Sun, so did a new faith radiate from the city in the mountains, and it left an indelible mark throughout Peru.

There are still great quantities of material buried beneath the rubble and much remains a mystery. William H. Prescott, writing his great *History of the Conquest of Peru* in 1847, described Tiahuanaco as "a land of darkness that lies far beyond the domain of history," and his verdict still stands, although so much has been brought to light since he wrote. All we know for certain is that the rulers of Tiahuanaco, like the Incas after them, set their stamp on the character of the country. They created a "horizon," as the archaeologists say.

Was this the first "horizon," the first cult or culture, which affected the whole of Peru?

This was the question asked by the greatest Peruvian archaeologist, Julio Tello, who explored the whole of his native land. He searched throughout the country and everywhere he came across remains which were reminiscent of Tiahuanaco. In Huari, which lies in the province of Ayacucho, Tello found ruins covering an area of four square miles, where the walls were once twenty-five feet high. Stone figures were unearthed almost everywhere and in Pucara alone there were twenty-one of them, to say nothing of sixteen monoliths and forty-eight blocks with relief carvings. These carvings depicted hybrid creatures—part human and part jaguar, condor, llama, or fish—and the temples they had once adorned were built in the shape of a horseshoe. At Pisco on the southern coast, a region where adobe brick was universal, Tello discovered the ruins of two towns built of stone, which had been founded long before the reign of the three "world-changers," the great Inca emperors Pachacuti, Tupac Yupanqui, and Huayna Capac. In fact, he came across Tiahuanaco influence throughout the length and breadth of Peru, north and south, east and west.

In the highlands and in the coastal valleys, he found traces of the Amauta and he had no doubt at all that Pirua had become an empire. But what kept him guessing all his life was this: Was the Pirua the oldest Peruvian empire? Or was there not an earlier "horizon," one which preceded Tiahuanaco?

Tello went on looking until he found the answer. He delved more deeply into ancient times than anyone had done before him. And one day there lay before him the earliest horizon of them all.

The earliest horizon

One of the first Spaniards to come to Peru was the young officer Pedro de Cieza de León. He rode on horseback to find out what he could about the land and on one of his rides he came to a place which lay in an upland valley hundreds of miles to the north of Tiahuanaco. It was a shrine famous for its temples, and the ruins of them are still standing today. No one knew how old they were at the time of the Spanish Conquest, but pilgrims flocked there year after year and not only Cieza but other historians confirm that the place was as famous throughout Peru "as Rome or Jerusalem with us."

We can still see from the remains what a mighty city it was that once stood there. There was a central court and around it were three-tiered buildings on square pyramid foundations which were faced with stone blocks. Huge figureheads were secured to the walls with strong tenons, the heads of gods with tusks at the corners of their mouths. A granite staircase led to a gateway in the middle story, but apart from this there was no entrance, not even a window, although every room was ventilated by means of shafts.

Just as in Tiahuanaco the temple and the lake were connected by a stairway, so this temple was linked with the River Puccha which flowed through the valley. Broad steps rose from its bank up the slope to where the temple stood. The inside was a maze of windowless passages, chambers, and alcoves just high enough for a man to stand upright and lined with small square stones. On the highest tier was a basin of hard black stone which stood on heavy feet. It was designed to receive the blood of the sacrifice. The blood flowed down from the stone altar along a gutter and so to a block of stone where a jaguar lifted its stone face.

Not far from the ruins, there is a village called Chavín de Huantar. *Chavín* is a Colla word which means "in the bush." The temple itself lies in an inhospitable valley where there is little soil for cultivation and not much space to lay out fields. Unlike Tiahuanaco, the builders of Chavín relied on the collaboration of the pilgrims who came to worship there. Wendell Bennett declared that the plan on which Chavín was built must have been decided beforehand down to the last detail. True, there were temple workshops in Chavín, but assistance came from the nation as a whole, for pilgrims must have arrived in their thousands, just as today they flock to the holy places in Peru on saints' days. So there must have been streams of pilgrims making for the shrine at Chavín de Huantar for the ritual sacrifices and they may have stayed for several weeks at a time. When sufficient numbers were assembled, building materials were transported to the site, the foundations were laid, and the slabs were put into place. When the festivities were over, the pilgrims returned to their distant homes and professional builders, stone masons, and sculptors, with some help from the local population, completed what the pilgrims had begun.

Head of a god. Chavín

In 1873, the Peruvian scholar Raimondi discovered the famous green stone of Chavín de Huantar, the mysterious god who carries a tower of heads on his shoulders. Fifty years later, Julio Tello was working in the labyrinth when he discovered an unusually long, pointed piece of stone, rather like a gigantic dagger. When he examined it closely, he realized that it was in the form of a jaguar standing on its hind legs. It had two heads, one of which was set on top of the other like a helmet, and threatening fangs protruded from both its mouths. Thick strands of storm-tossed hair grew into the heads of snakes. This was the god of the Chavín, a sinister deity which reminds us of the Gorgon's head.

But Tello found that this god was not confined to Huantar. The jaguar head turned up everywhere in Peru among the oldest of the stone ruins. Raimondi's green stone had already stirred Tello's curiosity many years before, but once the jaguar god from the labyrinth had placed its paw on his shoulder, it never let him go again.

Tello knew Peru inside out, far better than anyone else

of his time. He was equally at home in the jungle, in the desert, and in the highlands. He had often witnessed for himself how the clouds from the jungle rise over the mountains, how they flash with lightning and break with a thunderclap over the Andes. The storm comes like a monstrous jaguar, bringing life with it, swelling the lakes and turning the rivers into mighty torrents which saw their way through the rock and split the desert asunder. In storm and rain the jaguar god comes with a roar, leaping through the window between the snow-covered peaks. It bares its pointed red fangs and lashes the land with its dripping paws and dripping tail until the countryside awakes and blossoms.

Tello did not think of the sea from which life arose as the Pacific in the west. He looked for it in the Amazon basin, in the vast uncharted jungle where the Iawa Indians live today. One of their myths goes like this:

In the beginning was the moon. It is so old that there is nothing older. As there was nothing else, the moon was quite alone, and to stop itself from feeling bored it created the jungle and mankind. Then it pleased the moon to look down on the earth, but soon it felt pity for mankind because they were surrounded by darkness all day, and there was no sun in the sky. The moon saw a beautiful Iawa girl and so it produced a jaguar out of itself and sent it down to the girl, who took the jaguar for her husband. They had a son who shone like gold, and from his birth the Iawa tribe worshipped him. When he was grown up he climbed onto a funeral pyre and set fire to it himself. And from the flames, the jaguar's son rose into the sky and became the sun. And so the Chavín god is the jaguar who comes from the moon and carries the sun within himself.

Chavín de Huantar is probably the oldest of the stone temples yet discovered in Peru. Its main sector, which the Spaniards called the Castillo, measures 245 by 235 feet along the base. In 1945 it was almost wholly destroyed by an earth-

169

quake, but it is certain that the building followed the three-tiered pattern. Another Chavín pyramid, which was discovered near a tributary of the River Jequetepeque, was also three-tiered. It was called Kuntur Huasi, the house of the condor. It contains many Chavín reliefs carved on flat stones, and golden ornaments have been discovered in tombs around the pyramid.

The richest Chavín finds on the northern part of the coast were made by Larco Hoyle. In the Chicama and neighboring valleys, he discovered whole towns of tombs. Rich funeral gifts were buried with the corpses—mirrors, ornaments, decorated stone platters, and bones. Vessels of various shapes were particularly numerous. There were jars, jugs, and bottles, egg-shaped and round, with the eyes or teeth of beasts of prey scratched on them. Many of these containers represent faces, animals, fruits, or whole figures. One jug portrays a vivid scene from everyday life. It is a mother suckling her child and she is gazing into space with huge eyes. A large shawl covers her head and back, and on her shoulders is a stirrup handle and a spout from which the life-giving water pours forth.

The color of life was placed in the grave too. It took the form of red dust which was sprinkled on the body and penetrated right through to the bone.

Tello found middens with Chavín remains in the central coast as well, and Rebeca Carrión Cachot traced Chavín features on early Paracas pottery. This lady continued Tello's work when he died, and she firmly believed that at the time of the Chavín culture the people of Paracas were busy clearing away the sand of the desert until they reached moist soil, the banks of subterranean rivers where they created their gardens. Not far from the big necropolis which Tello discovered in 1923, where he found more than four hundred

Highland Indian woman with unmistakably Mongolian features

Jaguar god of the Chavín

mummies all wrapped in splendid shrouds, another digging took place in 1952 and straw roofs were found in the sand, the remains of oases which these resourceful people had been able to detect in the "basement" of the desert thousands of years ago. Reservoirs have been found near Lima which prove that the Chavín people certainly knew how to conserve their water supplies.

Twenty-five sites with Chavín ruins or tombs have been confirmed to date. The most important of them are in the Nepeña Valley. They are Cerro Blanco and Punkuri, and Tello discovered them in the nineteen-thirties. He found walls in Cerro Blanco with clay reliefs which had red and yellow-green eyes. In Punkuri he found a wild animal's head made of clay and stone. It was keeping watch over a concealed grave.

In the Casma Valley, too, explorers discovered the remains of pyramids which were reminiscent of Chavín style. One of them, Cerro Sechin, is particularly puzzling. It is surrounded by stone columns on which figures are carved. Some are warriors with hats on their heads, loincloths around their hips, and clubs in their hands. The people standing near them are unarmed and they look as if they are awaiting the end. One

Stone column of Cerro Sechin

of them has already been decapitated by a blow. Their features are distorted with fear, their hands are frozen, their
hair stands on end in thick strands. Many archaeologists
think that Cerro Sechin was a forerunner of Chavín, but the
figures fit in very well with the "horizon" style which Tello
discovered.

Reliefs and clay vessels from the Chavín times tell little of
how the people lived. Most of the jars are dark, self-colored,
and covered with decorations like jungle creepers. The lines
look as though a jaguar had scratched them with its claws.
Only a few of the vessels show faces or human figures and
there is something sinister about them all. The houses
scratched on the vessels enable us to guess that the Chavín

172

people lived in thatched huts with walls of mud or fieldstone. Their clothing too was of the simplest. In the coastal regions the main item was the loincloth.

Many crops were cultivated, such as manioc, peanuts, peppers and gourds, and above all corn. Corn appeared in Peru at the same time as the jaguar god. Fertile soil was sacred and nothing was built on it. Often it is only the refuse heaps which reveal where a settlement once stood, well away from the cultivated land. Indians have never been afraid of traveling long distances. In the history of a king named Yampellec it is related that the immigrants went to seek their ruler after he had taken wings from heaven and flown away. The seekers remained "there where they heard the voice of their king," but they often felt themselves called to leave a place and the Chavín people were no different. To resist a call was dangerous. The jaguar god flashed his eyes and showed them the way. He was a god who struck again and again.

Through the constant menace of his surroundings, the Indian was compelled to fight back all the time. The world of rock and desert threatened him with starvation, so he terraced the ground and cultivated it. The dry river beds threatened him with death from thirst, so he built reservoirs and canals. Torrential floods threatened to wash his house and his fields into the sea, so the Chavín built the first dams. He wrested from the forces of nature whatever he needed to survive, and in doing so he created life for himself. He shaped earthenware vessels; he made headbands and bracelets. He sharpened little sticks to pierce his ear lobes, he made rings for his fingers and tweezers forged of gold to pluck out his beard. He erected granite megaliths, and whatever he made was charged with such energy that no pottery, jewelry, or building of a later epoch can compete with it for dynamic power.

The jaguar god demanded sacrifices and the Chavín people offered up their produce, their animals—and themselves.

Wars were not fought for land in those days, since there was land enough, but for people whose blood would drench the altars, whose heads would be displayed as trophies. It was not without pride that the Chavín warrior laid before his god the head of the enemy he had killed, for it was a source of magic strength. By offering a life to his god, he demanded a longer life for himself in return.

Live sacrifices had not died out in Peru in Pizarro's time and even today in remote villages, animals are still brought to the old gods to be slaughtered. The Indio who acts as priest takes the heart of the llama while it is still beating and raises it high in the air as an offering to the sky.

Garcilaso de la Vega, the descendant of the Incas, whose father was a high court judge in the Inca capital of Cuzco, tells a story in his chronicle of an incident which happened in his father's day. There were already Catholic churches in Peru and the Spaniards celebrated all the festivals of the church with great pomp. The Indians took part in them

Beast-of-prey god holding a heart in his hand. Chavín relief

eagerly, for they loved festivals and now they were baptized. It was the feast of Corpus Christi and representatives of all the tribes came to take part in the procession in Cuzco. The sharply differentiated groups, each in their distinctive dress, approached the altars which were set up in all four quarters of the town. Suddenly, in front of one of the altars, a Cañari threw off his poncho, and everyone could see that he had a trophy head dangling from his girdle. The Indian swaggered boldly in front of the crucifix, displaying the severed head. The Spaniards froze in horror, but the Quechuas, who were the traditional enemies of the Cañaris, fell upon the man and would have killed him if the Spaniards had not intervened.

"How can the Spaniards allow these ancient feuds to be revived!" cried one of the Quechuas bitterly. The colonel-in-charge asked the man to explain. "This man fought on the side of the Spaniards when Cuzco was besieged by the rebel Inca," explained the Indian hotly. "During an attack, he killed the Quechua soldier whose head now hangs from his belt. Why should he flaunt it here when we are no longer at war with him?"

The Cañari had been badly manhandled, but he spoke up bravely: "I am prouder of taking this head than of anything else I have done in my life. For it tells me, 'You were the victor, I the conquered. You have your own life still and you have mine into the bargain.'" Again the Quechuas could only be held back with difficulty. They were ready to murder the Cañari, and their headman, who was beside himself with rage, declared, "It was not he who defeated our fellow tribesman. It was the new God who conquered, the one who came with the Spaniards!" And turning to the Cañari he shouted, "You know perfectly well that we only gave up the siege because this new God of the Christians is invincible, because he is more powerful than Viracocha and Pachacamac put together. We withdrew because we saw the miracles which he made the Spaniards perform—yes, every one of them!"

175

The Cañari said no more. He took the trophy head from his belt and placed it on the altar. That ended the quarrel, for now the Quechuas were satisfied. Their slaughtered compatriot had been brought as a sacrifice and that was the noblest destiny which could overtake a man. Those who were sacrificed became part of the divinity, their lives went into the god to give him strength and to spread his dominion over others.

The god of the Chavín was lord in his kingdom, which was obviously not created through wars like the empire of the Incas. Weapons are seldom found in Chavín tombs. The jaguar god needed no armies to conquer for him. Missionaries paved the way instead. Scholars can read this from their finds. A map drawn up of all the Chavín buildings discovered so far would comprise every region of Peru, and the Chavín god was the first unifying force in the country.

His was the strength of a primal force, but nowhere did he destroy. When we look at the building, the carvings, and the pottery of this epoch, it is at once apparent that here was a god to grip the minds of men. His power can be seen in the characteristic bold curves of Chavín art. It is the same power which we feel when we look at primitive cave drawings. The strongest pictures are always the oldest ones, the ones at the beginning. When there is no security, when danger threatens everywhere, everything is demanded of human beings. The hunter in the Ice Age had to be on his guard all the time, never knowing when he might meet a mammoth or a mountain lion, a bison or a rhinoceros. The Chavín man knew that he was up against the most powerful forces, the menace of the desert, the jungle, and the naked mountains.

The sea, too, was part of the Chavín world and fish are often carved in their reliefs, including whales. This occurs not only in the coastal valleys but also in the highlands, just as, inversely, the llama crops up on the coast. Remains of sacrificial llamas are found frequently in the coastal graves, together with fragments from Chavín times.

This raises another question in its turn. Was the coastal strip the Land of the Dead for the early Peruvians? Was there for them, as for the Pharaohs, a land in the west where the silence of the desert received the dead? The roads between the sea and the *puna* do not betray any secrets.

Tello was convinced that the Chavín had their origin in the jungle and came down from the mountains to the coast. Uhle, the German archaeologist who was the first to dig systematically right across the country, found evidence which suggested that the first Chavín temple was by the sea. The two great scholars could not agree. Others were drawn into the controversy, but even today it is not decided, although some of the most recent discoveries support Uhle's interpretation.

There is in Mexico a city called Tlatilco, which is associated with an early religious cult, and fragments have been unearthed there which are almost identical with Chavín remains both in materials and design. Jugs with stirrup-spout handles and zigzag patterns are found in Mexico as well as in Peru. The beast of prey deity with the tusks was also known to the Olmeke, an ancient Mexican tribe. What is more, during the last few years archaeologists have found metalwork and pottery in the coastal plains of Ecuador which are closely related to the forms the Chavín used. Max Uhle's sharp eyes were the first to observe this "bridge" connecting the early Mexican cultures with the Chavín.

But Tello was not mistaken either when he saw the life-giving god of the Chavín in the breath of the jungle which steams over the land. The lines on Chavín vases twist and writhe just like jungle creepers.

Tello went as far back as six thousand years ago to find the beginnings of Chavín culture. He placed its high-water

mark at about 1500 B.C. Modern scientific tests tell us that
it was about 1000 B.C. that corn was first cultivated in Peru
and at about the same time, we know, there were arti-
cles being wrought in gold, and pottery, megaliths, and buildings which had all reached a degree of perfection for their
kind. Before that, clay was crudely shaped and not fired.
Baskets and textiles were of the simplest kind. How did it
come about that such techniques were acquired? How do the
historians account for such a leap forward in human skills?

The answer may lie in the immigrants who came as teachers and not as pupils. They moved in the spheres of pottery,

Cloth made from cotton. Inca style

masonry, and many other arts as sure of themselves as a bird through the air or a fish in the water. There are many myths which tell of the men who came from the north on their rafts. "Yampellec came with many people and brought with him a green stone around which a temple was built."

Research makes it more and more probable that the Chavín god came from over the sea with the wanderers. It is not only a jaguar but also a condor, and as in the plumed serpent of Mexico, it unites the features of the moon and the sun. In this deity are found all the signs which can be attributed, although with variations, to the later god of Tiahuanaco, as well as to the Inca god. It is a god which the Peruvians saw with different eyes at different epochs.

If Uhle was right, this divinity had already traveled some long distance across the sea before he became the godhead of the Peruvians. The multiple heads of the green stone of Chavín show clearly an origin in the distant past. It may well have been as distant geographically.

The turret of heads asks the question of the *huaca:* "From where do I come?"

To answer it we need to know what life was like before the Chavín era, and how the people lived in the earliest days, before they became Chavín worshippers, Tiahuanaco people, or Inca subjects. The rubbish heaps they left behind have survived from the time of the first settlements. What do the excavators find when they dig down to the deepest stratum of all?

The first and
the last discoverers

The Huaca Prieta was a rubbish heap which stood forty feet high on the right bank of the Chicama River. Junius Bird, the American explorer, found it a few decades ago, and when he dug through it he brought to light remains which went back to a time when corn, gold work, and pottery were quite unknown in the whole of Peru. After that, many "dark *huacas*" were thoroughly examined all along the coast, and in the past ten years a Frenchman, Frédéric Engel, has discovered another thirty such middens—and all on the coast. There must once have been "dark *huacas*" up in the highlands too, but there the remains must have rotted in the damper air and storms have probably washed them away from the stony ground. On the coast, the desert sand and the dry air have seen to it that even after five thousand years there are still rich finds awaiting the excavators, the latest discoverers of Peru.

Many archaeologists have delved deep in Peruvian prehistory and explored it right back to the start. Some famous

180

names are those of Bird, Engel, Bennett, Kroeber, Strong, and Larco Hoyle. What did they find in these heaps of debris, the castoffs of history, the things which men threw away when they became useless?

There are fishing hooks, and from this we know that the first settlers were fishermen. There are nets and the remains of boats which tell us that fishing did not take place only from the shore. Where the land is flat, the fishermen waded out to sea as they do today in many of the bays along the coast of Peru. Certain shells that are found only in deep waters indicate that these people were experienced divers; the bones of sea lions show they were resourceful hunters. The edges of their nets had floats of bottle gourds, while stones bored through the middle weighed down the center of the net and made sure that it hung down deep enough.

Bird discovered that people had lived in round caves which were roofed with whale bones and floored with pebbles. He ascertained that nets, pouches, and fabrics were made of a mixture of cotton and spurge fibers spun into irregular threads and clumsily knotted together. They decorated their cloth not only with zigzag patterns but also with snakes, cats, birds, and fishes, and they caught the nature of each creature so vividly that one can tell what they are at a glance.

Engel found slit tapestry, veils, and cloaks richly trimmed with feathers of brightly colored birds. There were necklaces of shells and pierced seeds, ear ornaments painted red, and mirrors of smoothly polished lava . . . It seems clear that man has been interested in adorning his person from the earliest times! The hunter painted himself before the hunt and in readiness for each feast.

Among the more important everyday utensils which were unearthed were hammer stones, scrapers, and flint knives. Fruits, meat, and fishes were roasted on hot stones and other foods were boiled in gourds, but because they were not fire-

181

proof, a method had to be used which demanded much patience. The cooking pot was placed by the side of the fire and hot stones were dropped into the water one by one until it was heated sufficiently to cook the food.

Most of the things which the coastal dwellers needed for survival came from the sea, but they were not only fishermen. They were settlers who laid out fields and had to wait for the harvest to ripen. Indeed, these earliest settled farmers were highly skilled. More than thirty useful crops were cultivated in Peru, and a number of our familiar foods originated or were developed there: peanuts, pineapples, cocoa, tomatoes, red peppers, some varieties of strawberries, and many kinds of beans. The highland Indians grew more than one hundred varieties of potato: white, yellow, brown, russet, and scarlet, sweet and sour, and they grew some which were frostproof and would thrive at a height of 16,000 feet. They also grew quinoa, a plant whose seeds were used as a cereal and which would mature even in the neighborhood of the glaciers. These earliest farmers certainly knew how to get the better of nature.

For thousands of years they lived in the traditional way until the introduction of corn into their world. Corn is a prolific crop, and in many districts of Yucatan and in Peru as well, corn farmers need work for only fifty days in the year in order to feed themselves and their families. The first corn farmers built the first brick houses in America and they also made the first earthenware vessels, which were shaped like pumpkins but pointed at the bottom so that they could be pushed into the soft earth and made to stand upright. They seldom decorated these jars and they did not fire them very well. Their tombs were simple too and the gifts laid with the bodies were meager. Often the pouch by the side of the dead contained nothing but a few grains or dried flowers.

But even before these early settlers, there were people

in Peru, as there were throughout the American continents. They were nomad hunters and Bird found their tracks even in the southernmost tip of Patagonia. As long ago as 8000 B.C. they were hunting the primitive bison, the ancestor of the horse, the guanaco, and the giant sloth. In Peru, Bird discovered secret hiding places where migrant hordes had left such objects as spear tips, blades, and scrapers, and stone tips at least ten thousand years old can be found all over America. The remains of a mastodon killed by hunters were discovered near Quito, and in 1952 in the Valley of Mexico, American explorers came across mammoth bones, and there were mallets, stone knives, and spear tips lying by their side. These early hunters used spear throwers and they rubbed certain woods together to make a fire and so frighten away the mammoth, the primitive horse, and the bison. Great water hogs, armadillos, and giant turtles were common in those days, and indeed, America remained a paradise for plants and animals later than any other continent.

And how did man arrive, an intruder in this paradise?

Antonio de la Calancha makes the following observation in his chronicle, published in 1638: "The people who in-

Rock drawing showing a shepherd with his llama flock

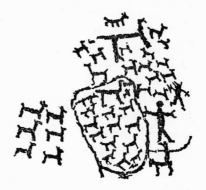

habited the Americas were Tartars, an aggressive people with the urge to conquer foreign lands and to force their dominion over others. With conquest as their aim, they set out from Asia and penetrated as far as Peru. They went from Tartary to Estotilandia [a mythical land in America, supposedly near the Arctic Circle] and they journeyed ninety degrees from west to east, that is, 1,575 Spanish leagues. From this point to Lima is another ninety degrees from north to south. Altogether it was a journey of 3,150 Spanish leagues, and if they marched at a steady seven leagues a day, they could have covered the distance from Tartary to Lima in four hundred and fifty days, even in difficult conditions."

So much for Father Antonio de la Calancha. He was probably right when he described the path of their journey, but he was sadly mistaken if he really believed that a distance like that could have been covered in such a ridiculously short time. Nor was he wrong in speaking of Tartary, for even today Mongolian features are widespread among the Indians. Calancha was right too when he said that they came on foot, for these early hunters who were the first to drift across the American continent came at a time when America and Asia were joined together. Great masses of ice held back the oceans and the sea was hundreds of fathoms below its present level. In the north, an isthmus connected Siberia with Alaska, and although the immigrants had to cross the ice barrier as they tracked the herds of bison and mammoth, there was no sea to stop them. So hordes of long-headed, beardless, slit-eyed Mongolians with stone axes, cudgels, and spears arrived in North America. Only it took them several thousand years to reach "Lima"! They have left their marks in Alaska as well as in the south, and in 1947 a complete human skeleton was found near Tepexpán in Mexico side by side with the remains of an elephant. In Nicaragua, the footprints of seventeen men were uncovered near those of a bison.

184

These tracks had been buried under lava and they were as clear "as on the first day."

And how far back was that "first day" when the Asiatic hunters tracked the first bison on American soil? It was thousands of years ago, we know, but whether it was twelve, fifteen, or even more, no one can say for certain yet. A few thousand years more or less are not vital in this context, however. The important factor is the way they came, and it was a long journey by any reckoning.

From the earliest times, man has been a wanderer, always driven by hunger and fear, and at the same time magically lured by the unknown. The early hunters were born explorers, always thirsty for new adventures. They shook their constant fears from them like wolves whose fur has been drenched to the skin. They were always trying to escape from boredom, always driven by the urge to attack a new

Rock drawing of Toro Muerto

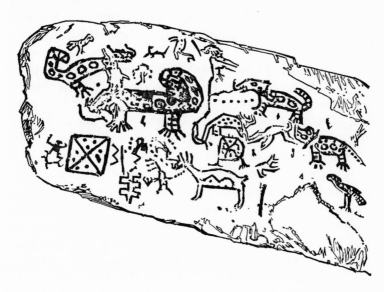

goal, to discover something fresh. So they searched as they hunted, and collected plants and seeds as they went. These hunters have scattered their spear tips and their knives throughout the length and breadth of a continent.

The strongest weapon of these earliest immigrants was their ability to adapt themselves to new conditions, to the plains and the desert, the jungle and the bare mountains. They climbed the Andes from the north. They found a world cleft by the wind, echoing with the thunder of falling avalanches, the subterranean rumble of volcanoes. They pressed forward into the *puna*, the great emptiness where everything seems dead and yet is bursting with life, dumb and eloquent at one and the same time. Here was a background where man could forget his fears. For here everything was dead, yet alive too.

There were once two brothers who lived in the *puna*. Each had a wife and children, but one was rich and the other poor. One day the rich man invited guests to a party. He was celebrating the day on which one of his sons was to have his hair cut short. It was a great event, for the boy would then receive the name he was to bear all his life, and of course the guests would bring him presents. There were gay goings-on in the rich man's house then, when the poor brother came to the door. The guests asked, "Who is there?" "Only one of my servants," declared the rich man in a loud voice. The poor man heard him and went away. A hole sprang in his breast and a black bird nested there. The bird spoke: "Your brother has disowned you. It would be only right and proper if you did the same." But the poor man could not bring himself to do that. As on other days, he went to look for herbs so that he could take some food back for his wife and children. But he stumbled along as if he were blind and he found nothing, neither berries nor roots nor herbs, and at last he had no strength left. He sat down by a great rock and said to the rock, "How is it possible that one

186

brother can disown another? Must this black bird live in my breast forever?"

Then the rock answered him: "Let the bird fly away! Listen to what the *puna* has to tell you. The *puna* says 'If your brother cuts himself off from you, he cuts away his own soul. A man can only harm himself like that. Come with me.' " So the man went with the *puna* and they met an old man who gave the poor man a stone and said, "When night overtakes you, knock against the earth with this stone wherever you are." The poor man set off in a hurry to reach home before nightfall but darkness overtook him near a hill. He knocked on the hill with the stone the old man had given him. Then he saw that there was a cave there. So he sat down in the cave, but he was so hungry that he did not know if he was alive or dead. He was so tired, too, that he did not know if he was awake or sleeping. "I have never been so terribly alone before," thought the poor brother. Then he heard the *puna* speaking once more. "Here is white broth for you," it said. Then the hill spoke. "Here is yellow broth for you," it said. "Here is red broth for you," said the cave and there were three dishes suddenly standing before the poor man, each of them steaming with broth. The poor man ate, and he left in each of the dishes enough for his wife and his children. Then he fell asleep.

When the sun woke him next day, he lifted the dishes from the ground and he saw that the white broth had become silver, the red broth copper, and the yellow broth pure gold. Now the poor man was rich and he returned to his home rejoicing. But his brother heard of the fortune and asked, "Where did you steal this copper, this silver, and this gold?" and the happy man told him of his adventure. As soon as the rich brother had heard every detail he went to find the old man and the cave. He too knocked with the stone, but the hill gave him only a shaggy pelt, the cave which opened for him presented him with horns, and the *puna* added a shaggy

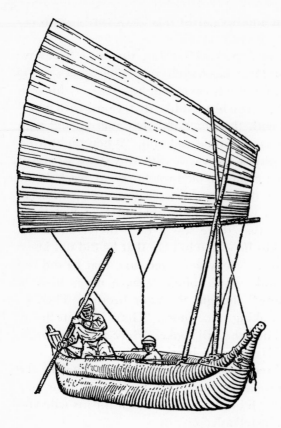

Boat with sail made from totora *reeds*

tail. When he returned home he had become an animal. No one recognized him, not even his sons, and since then he has wandered about the *puna*, homeless.

Everything in the *puna* is full of magic, everything is uncannily alive even if it seems to be dead. The Indians know it. Even today, magicians are greatly respected among them. In the oldest times, the magician was all-powerful. He could see through rocks and into the darkness. He could make the head of a sleeping man detach itself from his body, roll away, and then come back again. And when the sleeper awoke, he knew what his head had seen. The magician placed a spell on the rocks so that they should not invade the villages. He knew songs which could halt the hail in mid-air, and dances which would drive sickness from the huts. He could grasp the moon, for the moon was a boat in which he could sail from one side of the lake to the other. If he cast the right spell, a fish would become a bird, a stone would change into a man, and a fox would turn into a flame which leaped from stone to stone.

In the world of the early hunters, gods, men, animals, plants, heaven, and earth were all one. Anything could be changed into anything else. And things were lying in wait, so you had to be on your guard all the time. Only the wizard could see into things, and those on whom he bestowed his eyes. He could turn a shell or a little stone into a talisman. No one was safe unless he knew what kind of thing was waiting for him; and without the help of magic, early man felt lost. He shuddered at the great emptiness and he was afraid.

One day he found a reed with holes in it and he heard the wind blowing through it. So he took a reed for himself and blew through the holes. The void around him filled with notes, and things came to listen to him as he piped. They gathered around him and fear had no place there any longer. Thus the flute was discovered—in a reed. Others observed that the cacti had needles with which one could sew, that there were mats and roofing in the *ichu* grass, gum and firewood in the *algarrobo* tree, and boats and sails in the *totora* reeds. Step by step, the early people became inventors.

On the long way they had traveled they had learned what they must do to overcome their tiredness. They packed all their weariness into a stone. Then they put it in a place where others had left stones before them and so little cairns

189

grew up, signposts which said to the traveler: *You can follow this way, people have been here before.* The wanderers discovered that they were tireless, invincible. Nothing could stop them, neither ice nor storms, neither desert sands nor jungle nor naked rock. Bit by bit they learned how to defend themselves against evil. They traveled their long way and they stamped their features across a whole continent. The country of Peru fell into the hands of the earliest explorers as if it was theirs by right.

The archaeologists are their youngest brothers. They too are undeterred by snow and rain, by the dust and sand of the desert. Just as the hunters closed in to kill a mammoth or circled a herd of bison, so the archaeologists attack their many fields from many different angles. They are restoring to life Peru's buried civilizations, and that is why the country is more rightly theirs than it is the conquerors' of four hundred years ago, who came as destroyers, rigid in their iron armor and blind to everything that was not gold.

Admittedly gold has a magic gleam even for archaeol-

Rock drawing showing a figure, half man, half jaguar

ogists. There is feverish excitement on any dig if gold vessels, masks, and ornaments are brought to light. But often shreds of cloth, broken pottery, or faded feathers have a greater lure if they happen to be the key which can solve a riddle of the past. When Bird was digging in the Huaca Prieta, his great day came when he disinterred some fragments of bark. They must have come from trees in the jungle to the east, and this was the first actual proof that even in the earliest times there were communications right across Peru. The discovery of a parrot sanctuary near Nazca was further evidence to support this, and numerous finds have been made which point to the fact that the highlanders had colonies on the coast. In all the coastal valleys there are coffins of reeds containing llama blade-bones, so it seems that llamas were regarded as guides on the coast as well as in the mountains. Llamas led the dead through death.

In his memoirs, a scholar named Disselhoff relates an adventure which is highly symbolic. He once made a special journey from Arequipa to a place called Toro Muerto, in order to see a "picture book" which he had heard about from a Peruvian explorer. The "book" lay open in the desert for all to see, or rather it was strewn about on hundreds of slabs of rock. There were innumerable signs and pictures engraved on stone—circles, dots, animal heads, figures, and masks. There were foxes, lizards, and snakes, but the figure repeated most was that of the jaguar. Some of the pictures told a story. For instance, there was a herdsman casting a spell over his llamas so that they would follow him. Or a jaguar-man opening his breast like a window and lifting his paws. Disselhoff thought of Cerro Sachin, of the soldiers with their unarmed captives depicted on the Chavín column which Tello had discovered.

Soon Disselhoff was busy taking photographs. One striking picture had figures of men dancing, of snakes and a stag. He adjusted the lens, took one more look with his free eye—

191

Rock drawing of snakes, dancers, and a stag

and the pictures had vanished! They were gone as if a wet rag had wiped them away. Disselhoff stepped nearer, greatly puzzled. And as soon as his shadow fell across the stone, there were the picture stories again. The dancing men, the stag, and the snakes all emerged from the stone, conjured out of it by the explorer's shadow. The stone and the glare of the sun did not get along very well, so it seemed. They needed the intervention of the expert in order to come to life.

Many of the Peruvian rock drawings recall the ones in Valltorta in Spain, as well as those in the Sahara, Norway, and Siberia. Here as there, however, some of the stories they tell are written in a language which has hidden its message for thousands of years, and probably no one will ever be able to decipher them again and give them an authoritative interpretation.

But much of what was in deepest obscurity only a few decades ago has been cleared up in recent years and there are only useful comparisons to be made with finds outside the land of the Incas. Not far from Mexico City lies a lava field called Copilco and archaeologists have been sinking shafts through its surface, which is over thirty feet thick in places. The objects they are finding there hint at a culture which flourished four thousand years ago. In an Argentine valley, along a ten-mile stretch of wilderness, five thousand jars, dishes, and bottles were dug out of graves some fifteen to twenty feet below ground level. Today the valley is a haunted desert with only a dying tree to break the monotony here and there. Thousands of years ago there must have been settlements—and forests. A prosperous community flourished. Of all the five thousand objects disinterred, no two are alike. Only the motifs repeat themselves: jaguars and condors, circles, crosses, snakes, dancers with carnival sticks, and monkeys—smoking pipes! The geometric patterns and the strictly stylized animals remind one of the Kingdom of the Giants, and the "god of tears" depicted on so many of them is very like the carvings in Tiahuanaco.

But more questions remain open than answered; much lies hidden still in the soil of Peru. The field is still wide open for research. Today specialists come from all over the world, but more and more native Peruvians are joining their ranks, among them those who have Indian blood in their veins. One of them emerged as pre-eminent in his field. He was Julio César Tello, the pupil who overtook his teachers. More discoveries can be attributed to him than to any other excavator: about 82,000 objects in all. He led fifty expeditions to all parts of Peru and founded six museums. His most important contribution was his discovery of the Chavín culture. The passion for antiquity was awakened early in his life, when as a boy of ten he saw a trepanned skull where

Black pottery from La Cienega. North Argentina

the bone had been mended with gold. That one moment decided his life, and since that day he had only one ambition —to explore his country's past.

In fact, Tello acquired so much information that he could not record it all before he died and many facts went with him to the grave. He probed his country tirelessly, a modern descendant of those Ice Age hunters who became farmers and builders of cities on Peruvian soil. Treasure-trove seemed to draw him like a magnet. It seemed as if the objects themselves were telling him: *Dig here; this is worth while.* But even for Tello much remained unexplained and many later researches have proved that he was often wrong. Even for him some questions loomed up ahead like a brick wall.

One day, his friends asked him to tell them which he considered his greatest archaeological adventure. They thought it might be his discovery of the gold of Batán Grande or perhaps the superb textiles of Paracas. Instead, Tello began to speak about a rock.

194

Tello's story

It is just a rock, you would say, a large boulder like so many others in the *puna*. From the distance it looks as if a giant were sitting there, brooding, so lost in thought that he has forgotten to go on his way. It leans forward a little to make a kind of overhanging roof, so that herdsmen find shelter there, and llamas too, when they taste the ice in the *puna* wind. Sometimes a priest comes to visit it from far away, for this stone is unique. There is not another one like it in the whole country. It is one of the most important *huacas* in Peru.

The legend has it that Viracocha himself once emerged from this particular rock. It was here that he appeared to the boy herding his father's llamas, the prince who called himself Viracocha Inca later when he deposed his father. The prince had fallen asleep under the sheltering rock, and at dawn the god had wakened the prince to warn him that the kingdom was in danger. Since then, pilgrims have often come to spend the night there like the Inca prince, and they wait for the god to rouse them and to speak to them.

I had never visited the place before, but we were digging not far away and we had had no luck at all so far. In fact, I couldn't remember any previous expedition which had produced such poor results. But it was not that which depressed me. So many unanswered queries had accumulated inside me, the result of more than thirty years of excavation, that I felt discouraged, for many of these questions stuck in my flesh like barbed arrows and they would not let me go. That was what brought me to the Viracocha rock. After all, I thought, if he gave advice to the prince and since then to many others, why should he deny it to me? So I went. I set off toward evening, for it was not very far, less than a two hours' walk. But I was tired, and not only from a hard day's work. The nearer I came to the rock, the more hopeless I felt. Those barbed arrows had dug themselves in deeper than ever before, and I was beset by a host of doubts which had given me no peace for years. The twilight thickened. I had to keep my wits about me or I might have lost my way.

I kept thinking of the young prince whose father was the weeper of blood, and who had been sent up here to herd llamas as a punishment for breaking the images of the gods. How did I know about him? Who had told me? I racked my brains.

And suddenly there was a figure standing near me, an Indian wearing sixteenth-century Spanish dress. He was someone I had known for more than thirty years—Poma de Ayala, the Inca's great-grandson. "You can believe what I wrote," he said to me, "and the pictures in my book are all true. And what Garcilaso told you, too . . ."

But before I could answer a word, another shadow emerged. It was Sarmiento the Sailor. "I listened to witnesses for years on end," he said emphatically. "I can tell you what these Incas were really like better than their descendants who invented many things just to blacken the reputation of us Spaniards!"

I recognized Sarmiento at once, but then I looked him in the face and then turned back to Poma de Ayala, neither of them could return my gaze. They drew back and I went on my way with other questions bubbling inside me. Where had the tenth Inca gone, the one who had sailed westward, "to find out if his star still shone for him over the sea"? Where did he get the horse's skull and the throne of brass? When was it that the sun became mightier than the moon? Who erected the Gateway of the Sun and who destroyed it?

A priest overtook me, striding along with long steps. He began to talk of the kingdom of Pirua. "Pirua Manco founded the kingdom and it is called after him. And this first Amauta was not a servant of idols . . ."

"And Ophir was the first Peruvian," I finished the sentence for him. The padre stopped dead. He was not accustomed to being interrupted.

I was alone once more, and when I came to the boulder it was quite alone too. There were not even llamas in sight. I sat down and waited until the night grew black. Too many problems tormented me for me to go to sleep. In the dark I could see before me the green stone of Chavín, the turret of heads. *Huaca*—out of which I come. But where was that? How far back had I to go to find the beginning of the Chavín epoch? Where did Peru begin?

I had not the courage to ask the rock yet. I thought of old Montesinos and his fairy tales, and how I had offended him. He had never wrestled with doubt. For him, Ophir discovered Peru and that was that. But his list of the kings of Pirua still stood: "There were one hundred and two of them . . ." One of the later Amautas, Tupac Cauri, often puzzled me. If Montesinos was right, this was the Amauta who, like the Chinese emperor Shih Huang Ti, had had all written records carefully burned. If I tell the rock that story, I

197

Pouch with llama ornament. Inca period

thought, perhaps it will listen to me. Perhaps it will even talk to me if it cannot stand the silence any longer.

And so I began, quite out of the blue: "This Amauta, Tupac Cauri, called himself the seventh Pachacuti, after he succeeded in rebuilding the kingdom of Pirua. For many years he had been harried by hostile tribes from the south, but he had not been able to drive them away until the priests told him the reasons for his failure. 'It is because you allow even the common people to read,' they said. 'You must not allow them to write on leaves as is the custom everywhere these days. Only the initiated should be able to read. We will invent a writing for you which will be only for the few.' So they invented the knotted cords, and whatever had been written down was burned."

198

I pricked my ears to hear how the rock had received my tale. It said nothing. Perhaps it had not been listening. It hung heavily over me, blocking out a great slice of the sky. There seemed no point in telling it stories. So I wrapped myself in my cloak and fell asleep at last.

I did not dream. I lay there like a stone—until someone woke me up. I started up and realized that I was freezing cold. The night was no longer quite so black, and morning was in the air. I saw no one, only the rock. It looked strangely alive in the half-light.

"Did you wake me?" I asked it.

And then I saw the god. At first I could make out only the marks of tears at the corners of his eyes, but then I saw the large eyes themselves, deep in shadow. There in the stone was the face of Viracocha, unmistakably. The eyes were waiting for my questions, but I was so agitated that I had to rack my brains to think what to say.

"Who are you?" I blurted out at last. "How long have you existed?"

Rock drawing showing a figure with the sun for its head

The face in the rock looked at me with a stony stare as if it would never answer me.

"Why not?" I demanded. "Why do you refuse to answer me? I have searched for you for a lifetime and with far more passion than others who have had to come from far away." I was thinking of the Frenchmen, the Germans, and the scholars from the United States.

Then there was a voice. I heard it clearly: "Have you not come from farther still? Were not your ancestors subjects of the Incas? And what about their forefathers, the Chimu potters and the Chavín weavers? Look back beyond them. Were they not farmers, and before that hunters? Did you not come in the track of the bison herds? You have only to look inside yourself."

"Perhaps," I answered, and I was trembling with amazement. "Maybe that is why I have discovered these thousands of remains. Perhaps that is why these things speak to me . . . But all the same, they do not say enough," I protested. "And sometimes they tell lies."

A look silenced me for a moment. Then I went on more cautiously: "They say one thing to me but something different to someone else. How can that be?"

"The fault is not in the objects you find," came the answer.

I was so struck by this that I began to wonder if I was awake or dreaming. I grasped the stone. It was hard, cold, unyielding. Then I grew more vehement. "I have never spared myself," I told the rock. "I have dug and dug, doing as much as my strength would allow. I am ready to admit my mistakes. Only tell me where I am right and where I am wrong. That is all I want to know and I shall never stop asking until I am sure."

The rock shimmered in the first light of day. Viracocha's face was growing paler. The marks of his tears began to blur. I was seized with fear that he would escape me. "Give me an answer as you gave one to the llama herdsman. Do not withhold your counsel," I implored.

Then the rock revealed its secret to me and I heard a voice telling me what had really happened. "The Inca prince often came here because the rock sheltered him from the wind and the rain. The llamas crowded around him but he did not see them. He was alone with his emotions and the spell fell upon him. He was angry with his father for the kingdom was in danger, yet the Inca behaved as if there were no threat to his realm. But he, the prince, saw clearly that the Chancas were coming."

"Because you warned him," I said. "Because you appeared to him."

"You are right," said the voice. "It was because he needed me that he drew me out of the rock. He knew his father and he thought: Only if Viracocha sends me to him will he listen to me. And so he saw me in the rock. Before that, I was nothing but a stone out here in the *puna*. Only through the Inca prince did I become what I am now."

I stared at the boulder soberly. "So he had his knowledge from within himself and not from you?" I asked after a pause.

For the last time I heard the voice. "I spoke to him through himself, just as I do now with you," it declared. "Why should I not, seeing that I am a god?"

Now it was light. I could not make out the face any more. The sun burned its way into the sky. Daylight had arrived and everything was bathed in its glare. The *puna* was stirring. I was no longer cold and I walked back to the place where we were excavating.

Later that day we dug out an image of Viracocha, the god who had roused me at dawn at the foot of the rock.

Glossary

Brief Alphabetical Guide to Ancient Peru

Acllahuasi—The school for "chosen maidens," who were educated to become temple or palace servants or members of the Inca's harem.

Adobe—Bricks made of mud and dried in the sun. The shapes varied; consequently the age of a building can be told from them.

Amautas—The name given both to the kings of the legendary kingdom of Pirua and to the Inca's counselors, the "wise men" who were teachers in the schools for the sons of the nobles.

Apurimac—"The Great Speaker": the river on which Machu Picchu stands—the "lost city" whose ruins were discovered by Hiram Bingham in 1911.

Ayllu—The big family group or clan whose members considered themselves to be the descendants of a common ancestor, worshipped as their *huaca*. Fields and meadows were owned by the *ayllu* in common.

Aymará—An Indian tribe of the highlands, who live mainly

in the area of Lake Titicaca; presumably the original creators of the Tiahuanaco culture.

Balsa—Rafts and other floating craft made from balsa stalks, reeds, sedge, dried skins, or gourds. Reeds were rolled into cigar-shaped bundles and these were tied together, usually in fours, to make light boats which the Spaniards called *caballitos* (little horses). They were hauled ashore every night to dry out.

Borla—The red band or fillet which the Inca wore around his forehead as the symbol of his royalty.

Cajamarca—The capital of a small Indian kingdom in the northern highlands which was incorporated into the Inca realm about A.D. 1450. There are hot springs there. Twice in its history, Cajamarca witnessed the collection of fabulous treasure: first, after the Inca conquest of the Chimu kingdom, and second, when the Spaniards defeated Atahualpa.

Calendar—From the earliest times, astronomy played a part in the life of the Peruvians. We know this not only from the way they built their temples, erected "sun stones" or gnomon towers as they are called, and "scratched" enormous pictures out of the desert on the southern coast, but also from the myths which have been handed down from one generation to the next.

Camayoc—A lord or governor, one of the high officials in the Inca empire.

Cañari—An Indian tribe living in the highlands of what is now Ecuador. They fought bitterly to resist Inca domination, but when they were finally conquered, they were used to supply the Inca's bodyguard.

Central Andes Region—The area influenced in turn by the Chavín, the Tiahuanaco, and the Inca cultures at the time of their widest expansion. The archaeologist includes not only Peru in this definition but large tracts of Bolivia, Ecuador, and Chile.

Chasquis—The runners or couriers, the Inca's messengers and porters. Relays of *chasquis* carried news and short despatches as well as fresh fish and fruit from the coast to Cuzco. They ran at fantastic speeds and they announced their arrival by blowing on conch shells.

Chavín—The earliest of the known Peruvian cultures, whose influence penetrated almost everywhere in Peru. It probably started about 1000 B.C. The chief centers located so far are Chavín de Huantar, Kuntur Huasi, Cerro Blanco, and possibly Cerro Sechin as well. Its origins are disputed, but it was a widespread cult which produced striking buildings, pottery, and textiles. The ruling godhead had threatening features like a beast of prey. Chavín elements persisted in various forms right up to the Inca regime.

Chicha—Corn beer. It was customary for the women to half-chew the corn kernels and then spit them into a big pot to assist fermentation. Chicha was very popular in ancient Peru and was drunk in great quantities on feast days.

Chimu—The most important of the kingdoms on the Peruvian coast, which flourished from about A.D. 1200 to 1450. It was then included in the Inca empire. The capital was Chan-Chan (Snake City), which consisted of ten wards or sectors and was spread over an area of more than eight square miles.

Chincha—The southernmost of the "Little Kingdoms of the Coast."

Coca—The leaves of the coca plant were mixed with lime and chewed. They eased the pangs of hunger and relieved heart strain in the thin air of the mountains.

Colla—Indian tribes of the southern highlands.

Conquistadores—"The Conquerors." This name was given to the 168 Spaniards who, under Francisco Pizarro and his brothers, took possession of the realm of the Incas.

After preparing for many years, they made a daring advance into the heart of the kingdom and, in Cajamarca, they lured the last of the Incas into a trap and had him executed. Pizarro and his compatriot Almagro had an agreement to divide the enormous booty between them, but Pizarro fobbed off Almagro with the poorer, southern half of the empire. Almagro set off on his famous march into Chile and returned in the nick of time to rescue the Pizarro brothers who were being besieged both in Cuzco and in Lima. Almagro was executed on Pizarro's command, but in the eyes of many historians, Almagro was "the better man" of the two.

Coricancha—"The Golden House": the chief temple in Cuzco under the Incas where the gods were portrayed as golden images. In their midst was enthroned the highest deity of all, the Original Egg, the source of all life. A sketch of the "high altar" of Coricancha, drawn by the Indian Pachacuti Yamqui Salcamayhua, was found among the possessions left by one of the first Peruvian bishops who made a name for himself by suppressing the Indian religion.

Coya—The Inca's chief wife, the queen.

Cuismancu—The central kingdom of the "Little Kingdoms of the Coast."

Cultures—The epochs of the primitive hunters and the early farmers in Peru were followed by three cultures: first the Chavín, then the Tiahuanaco, and finally the Inca. These covered the whole country, but there were also astonishing achievements in many fields in more restricted areas such as Mochica, Paracas, Nazca, and Chimu, and these lasted for long periods. However, in spite of the wealth of archaeological finds, it is not yet possible to arrange these cultures in chronological order with complete certainty.

Curaca—One of the highest officials in the Inca empire.

The name was also given as a title to the conquered princes of formerly independent territories.

Curuchec—"That which makes to flow": the Quechua word for lead, which was used for smelting silver.

Cuzco—"The fourfold": the Inca capital, which was divided roughly into four sections. The upper city was known as Hurin, the lower one as Hanan. It had great temples and palaces, but these were destroyed in 1535 in a battle between the Inca people and the Spaniards. Afterwards the city was rebuilt from the ruins, and subsequent earthquakes, especially that of 1950, have brought to light remains of the old Inca walls, still intact.

Gnomon towers—Columns or pillars used in observing the sun's meridian altitude.

Guano—Bird droppings used as fertilizer which can increase the yield of crops as much as thirty times over.

Hailli!—"Victory!": the cheer of the Inca people.

Huaca—A sanctuary or shrine. Later the word was used loosely for any excavation site as well as for the objects found in diggings. Literally, it means "out of which I come" and it denoted the original founder of a clan who, when he died, returned to the place of his birth and was changed into a tree, a stone, or an animal.

Huaca del Sol—The Pyramid of the Sun near Trujillo. It had five tiers, and was 250 yards long, 100 yards wide, and 50 yards high. It is estimated that nearly thirteen million adobe bricks, rectangular in shape, were used in its construction. Not far from it was the six-tiered Pyramid of the Moon, and the ruins of the temple on its base have frescoes on their walls. These pyramid temples were erected at the time of the Mochica culture.

Huaca Prieta—An excavation site near the mouth of the Chicama River, on the northern coast of Peru. In 1946 traces of a very early settlement were discovered here

206

and it was possible to compile a chronological table of its history going back almost to 3000 B.C.

Huacha Cupac—"Protector of the unfortunate": a title of honor for the queen.

Huaqueros—Treasure seekers, grave robbers, "collectors"— an army of unscrupulous and destructive fortune hunters who have preyed on Peru for many centuries.

Ichu—Mountain grass.

Ichuri—The priests who received the confession of sinners under the Incas.

Inca(s)—The Spaniards used the word "Inca" to denote not only the Quechua tribe but all Indian tribes who had been subjects of the Inca empire. Strictly speaking, the word applies to the *ayllu* or clan of the ruling house or dynasty, and the thirteen rulers known as "the Incas of Peru" are as follows: Manco Capac, Sinchi Roca, Loque Yupanqui, Mayta Capac, Capac Yupanqui, Inca Roca, Yahuar Huacac, Viracocha Inca, Pachacuti, Tupac Yupanqui, Huayna Capac, Huáscar, and Atahualpa. The great empire builders were Pachacuti (1438-71), Tupac Yupanqui (1471-92), and Huayna Capac (1492-1527). After five years of civil war, Atahualpa defeated the lawful heir, Huáscar. The Incas were emperors, warriors, and statesmen, who were convinced of their mission. Their extensive empire was built in less than one hundred years. By a policy which combined the suppression of political independence with cultural tolerance, they succeeded in creating the largest power block in the Americas prior to the Spanish Conquest.

Inti—The sun or the Sun God.

Intihuatana—"The stone of the sun," the gnomon tower or column which was "tied" to the sun by "magic" at the turn of the year (the solstice).

Inti Raymi—The festival of the Sun.

Llamas, etc.—The llama, alpaca, guanaco, and vicuña are known as "the camels of the Andes." The llama and the alpaca were domesticated in very early times and used as pack animals and for their wool, as well as for sacrifices. In the reign of the Incas, great drives or hunts were organized to capture the guanaco and vicuña.

Machu Picchu—"The lost city" of the Incas, about sixty miles from Cuzco, which was discovered in 1911 by Hiram Bingham.

Malqui—"Fruit-bearing tree." The name given to the mummies of former Incas, which were displayed at feasts. They continued to "reign" from the palaces they had occupied during their lifetime.

Mamacuna—The head of the *acllahuasi*, the school for "chosen maidens."

Mamanchic—"Our mother," a term of respect for the queen.

Manto—A cloak or wrapper. The most famous were those used as shrouds for the dead found at the Paracas necropolis.

Megalith—A large stone, usually set up as a monument.

Mitimaes—"Soldier settlers." Whole village communities were forcibly resettled to maintain dominion over conquered territories and to build agricultural terraces, roads, bridges, fortresses, and waterworks. Reliable citizens were removed to troubled districts and less trustworthy groups were moved into more stable communities.

Mochica—A civilization on the northern coast, a forerunner of the Chimu.

Monolith—A single block of stone such as a pillar or a memorial column.

Musical instruments—These included drums, rattles, bells, shells, cymbals, Panpipes, and other reeds. There were no stringed instruments. There are countless pictures to show that music and dancing were very popular. The potters even made jars which gave out "music" as they poured and whistling pots which looked as if they were alive and could use their lungs.

Nazca—A culture on the southern coast, contemporary with Mochica. Typical Nazca products are brightly colored ceramics and textiles.

Orejón—"Big ears," the name the Spaniards gave to the ruling caste in the Inca kingdom. As a sign of their rank they wore massive ear ornaments which distended the ear lobes.

Paccari Tampu—The place where the Incas were supposed to have originated.

Pachacamac—"Keeper of the world," the most exalted god on the coast, an oracle whose shrine of the same name was a traditional place of pilgrimage, even after the Inca conquest.

Pachamama—"Earth Mother," the Inca earth goddess.

Paracas—A peninsula on the southern coast, an almost rainless desert in which more than one necropolis has been found. The dead were placed in deep shafts and wrapped in *mantos* of great beauty. Until recently, historians made a distinction between two epochs, those of the Paracas Cavernas and the Paracas Necropolis, but Strong found evidence of an earlier period still ("Juan Palo") and at least one later one, so that a more precise definition may be forthcoming eventually.

Peru—A country hemmed in by sea, desert, and jungle, where the mountains and the flat coastal strip lie side by side. The inhospitable desert coast has virtually no rainfall, but it is pierced by about twenty-five rivers which make long ribbons of fertile oasis through the desert. Before Pizarro, Peru was a world where the wheel in any form, including the potter's wheel, was quite unknown, where there were no horses or cows, no milk and no glass. It was uninhabited until about 10,000 B.C. The first settlers came overland from the north and a second wave arrived from across the sea, also from the north. From about 1000 B.C. onwards, various cultures emerged, some of which overlapped or existed side by side, and others succeeded them. The inhabitants achieved high levels in many fields of the arts, especially in ceramics, weaving, working in gold, architecture, farming, and civil engineering—waterworks, roads, and bridges—and also in the realm of political organization. When the Spaniards discovered Peru, many of the remote areas were more accessible and the country better administered than it is today.

Peru is probably derived from the name of the River Biru, although some scholars think it may come from Pirua, a legendary kingdom supposed to have existed in the early days.

Pirca—A mixture of corn husks, mud, and pebbles which was used for surfacing roads.

Pucara—A fortress.

Puna—Bleak grasslands high in the mountains.

Punucrucu—"Frail sleeper": the Quechua term describing an old man who had reached the age of sixty.

Puric—The able-bodied worker, the ordinary citizen in the world of the Incas. There was one overseer for every ten *purics,* one over every hundred and every thousand. Over each ten thousand was a *tucui-ru-cuc,* "one who sees all." At the head of each of the four quarters of the Inca kingdom stood an Apu Capac ("His Excellency"), and above them, like a god, reigned the Inca.

Quechua—The Inca people who, between A.D. 1200 and 1500, conquered the whole of Peru as well as large portions of Ecuador, Bolivia, and Argentina. Also, the language of this people.

Quipu—Knotted cords used for keeping records, especially numerical ones. According to Poma de Ayala and other chroniclers, they also noted bulletins, laws, and even poems. Probably they served as mnemonics. Be that as it may, the *quipu* reader (the *quipucamayoc*) received a thorough education. Some historians take the view that there were attempts at a pictographic writing in Peru, apart from the knotted records, but the evidence for this is not conclusive.

Rimac—"The Speaker": the oracle god, forerunner of the god Pachacamac. It is also the name of the river from which Lima derives its name.

Runa Simi—"The human tongue": the Inca term for the Quechua language.

Sacsahuamán—A fortress near Cuzco with triple walls of Cyclopean proportions. Juan Pizarro, Francisco's brother, was killed storming the fortress in 1536.

Tawantinsuyu—"The Four Quarters (of the World)": the Incas' name for their empire.

Tampu (or Tambo)—A resthouse on the Inca road system. There were two immense networks of roads, interconnected at many points, which enabled communications to be maintained throughout the whole length and breadth of the Inca kingdom. This network, with its bridges, dams, and stairways up the mountainsides, is considered in both its extent and its construction to surpass even the roads of the Roman Empire.

Tiahuanaco—An early culture which had its center on the southern bank of Lake Titicaca, but exercised an extensive influence throughout Peru. It is typified by massive structures, among them the famous Gateway of the Sun, and by pottery and textiles severe in design but very beautiful. More has been written (and more nonsense, too!) about the ruins of Tiahuanaco than about any others either in the old or the new world.

Totora—Reeds from which boats, sails, thatches, and mats were and are made.

Trepanning—An operation for removing part of the skull, a

technique widely practiced in ancient Peru. It was performed not only for surgical reasons, but also to drive out evil spirits and to counter emanations believed to come from other worlds. The head was considered the home of magic powers. There were also operations to lengthen or flatten the shape of the skull. The dead were given vessels in the form of heads to protect them against evil. Heads taken as trophies exercised magical protection and increased the strength of the possessor.

Uru—The aborigines of Lake Titicaca. The tribute demanded from them by the tenth Inca was a "horn filled with lice" for each settlement. Remnants of the tribe still live on reeded islands in the lake today.

Villac-Uma—"Guardian of posterity": the High Priest of the Incas, who came next to the monarch in rank.

Viracocha—"The Earth-maker": the creator god in Tiahuanaco times, later introduced, like Pachacamac, into the Inca pantheon.

Yanacuna—"The Black Servants": members of a tribe which rebelled against the Inca but were pardoned on the inter-

Jar in the shape of a head with the lips held together with thorns. Nazca period

vention of the queen. Although these people did not
figure on any lists of citizens, they were often trained for
service at the Inca's court.

Yunca—Term used for the inhabitants of the Peruvian
coastal strip, as opposed to the Incas, who were essen-
tially highlanders. The term is also used for the land
itself. The Yunca world produced several cultures, including Mochica and Chimu, Paracas and Nazca, as well
as coastal Chavín and coastal Tiahuanaco—unless, after
all, Chavín did not find an outlet on the coast. This, like
so much else in Peru, is something which research has
still to clear up.

DATE	PERIOD	CULTURES					
		Northern | Central | Southern Coast			Northern | Central | Southern Highlands		
A.D. 1532 1438	Imperialists	Inca Empire					
1438 1250	Builders of Cities	Chimu	Cuismancu (Chancay)	Chincha (Ica)	Huamachuco	Inca	Collao
1250 1000	Expansionists	Coastal Tiahuanaco			Highland Tiahuanaco		
1000 400	Master Craftsmen	Mohica	Early Lima	Nazca Paracas Necropolis	Recuay	Tiahuanaco	
A.D. 400 B.C. 400	Experimentalists	Gallinazo Salinar	White-on-red	Paracas Cavernas	Huaraz	Chanapata	Chiripa
400 1000	Cultist Craftsmen	Coastal Chavín			Highland Chavín		
1000 3000	Early Farmers	Developing into settled communities					
3000 10,000	Early Hunters	Acquisition of Land					

This chart is based on the catalogue to the 1959 Cologne Exhibition "Treasures of Peru," with further additions by Dr. Haberland of the Ethnological Museum, Hamburg. The column "Distinctive art forms" is reproduced from *Altamerika* by Disselhoff and Linne (Baden-Baden, 1960).

There are, however, eminent Peruvian scholars who prefer a different chronology, such as the following used by Rebeca Carrión Cachot:

4000 B.C.–2000 B.C. Chavín
2000 B.C.–1000 B.C. Tiahuanaco-Paracas-Callao   A.D. 400–A.D. 1000 Chimu
1000 B.C.–A.D. 400 Mochica-Nazca   A.D. 1000–A.D. 1532 Inca

POLITICAL AND RELIGIOUS LIFE	HANDICRAFTS, ETC.	PLANTS CULTIVATED, FARMING TECHNIQUES, ETC.	DISTINCTIVE ART FORMS
Inca "Horizon" Centralized government Sun worship	Road construction Stone buildings		
Little kingdoms, especially along the coast	Mass production Bronze		
Tiahuanaco "Horizon"	Tiahuanaco style		
Caste system Animal demons worshipped	Arts and handicrafts at their best Massive buildings	Potatoes Sweet potatoes Oca lupine	
Development of various cultures, often restricted to a single valley	Copper, gold, silver, alloys Paracas textiles	Quinoa Black beans	
Chavín "Horizon" Stonebuilt cult centers	Gold Jaguar motif Stone sculptures	Peanuts Manioc Artificial irrigation	
Settlements of mud huts Primitive agriculture	Simple pottery Weaving Highly developed stone implements	Corn Beans Peppers Cotton Llama domesticated	
Hunting Fishing Gathering wild plants for food and sowing	Bone implements Plaiting Knotting Crude stone tools and weapons		

This is necessarily an oversimplified picture and most of the cultural periods described are much more complex than can be shown here. For example, the Tiahuanaco "Horizon" comprises the following cultures, so far as we can tell from the information available at present: Epigonic Mochica, Middle Ancon, Late Nazca, Wilkawain, and Huari. Nevertheless, between the years A.D. 1000–1250, they were all so deeply influenced by Tiahuanaco that one has no hesitation in speaking of one single "horizon."

CHRONICLERS AND EXPLORERS
OF PERU

CHRONICLERS: Antonio de la Calancha, Juan de Betanzos, Pedro
Cieza de León, Bernabé Cobo, Miguel de Estete, Garcilaso de la
Vega, Cristóbal de Molina, Fernando Montesinos, Pachacuti-Yam-
qui Salcamayhua, Hernando Pizarro, Pedro Pizarro, Juan Polo de
Ondegardo, Felipe Huamán Poma de Ayala, Pedro Sarmiento de
Gamboa, Francisco de Toledo.
EXPLORERS: Arthur Baessler, Louis Baudin, Wendell C. Bennett,
Hiram Bingham, Junius B. Bird, William Boyd, G. H. S. Bushnell,
Rebeca Carrión Cachot, Heinrich Cunow, H. D. Disselhoff, Hein-
rich Ubbelohde Doering, Frédéric Engel, Clifford Evans, Otfrid
von Hanstein, Raoul d'Harcourt, Robert von Heine-Geldern, Rafael
Karsten, Walter Krickeberg, A. L. Kroeber, George Kubler, Gerdt
Kutscher, Rafael Larco Herrera, Rafael Larco Hoyle, S. K. Lothrop,
Sir Clements R. Markham, J. Alden Mason, Norbert Mayrock,
Charles W. Mead, Philip A. Means, E. W. Middendorf, Jorge
Muelle, Baron E. Nordenskjöld, Arthur Posnansky, William H.
Prescott, Maria Reiche, Paul Rivet, John H. Rowe, Stig Rydén,
Eduard Seler, E. G. Squier, William D. Strong, Julio C. Tello,
Hermann Trimborn, J. J. von Tschudi, Max Uhle, Luis E. Valcar-
cel, Charles Wiener, Gordon Willey.

216

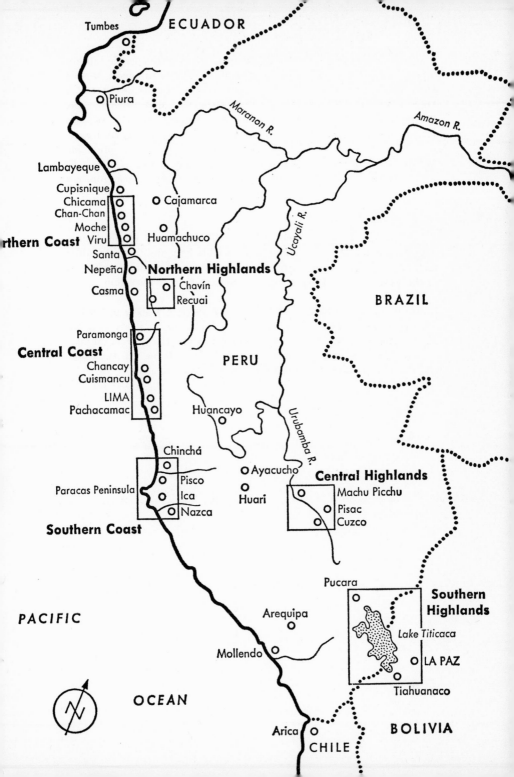

For help received in regard to both text and illustrations the author acknowledges his debt to the following books: Hiram Bingham, *Machu-Picchu*, London, 1930. G. H. S. Bushnell, *Ancient Peoples of the Andes*, Harmondsworth, 1949. H. D. Disselhoff, *Altamerika*, Baden-Baden, 1960. Bertrand Flornoy, *Rätselhaftes Inkareich*, Zürich, 1956. V. W. von Hagen, *Highway of the Sun*, London, 1955. Siegfried Huber, *Im Reiche der Inkas*, Olten and Freiburg, 1956. Gerdt Kutscher, *Chimu, eine indianische Hochkultur*, Berlin, 1950. Hermann Leicht, *Indianische Kunst und Kultur*, Zürich, 1944. F. H. Poma de Ayala, *Nueva crónica y buen gobierno*, Paris, 1936. Hermann Trimborn, *Das alte Amerika*, Zürich, 1959.

The author is specially indebted to Dr. W. Haberland of the Ethnological Museum, Hamburg, for much valuable help and for his reading and criticism of the manuscript. Thanks are due also to Dr. Otto Zerries of the Ethnological Museum, Munich, for his kind co-operation.

COLOR PHOTOGRAPHS: Martin Schliessler (4, 5, 6 above, 7, 8 above and below, 9, 10, 11, 13, 14, 15 above and below, 16, 17, 19, 20 below, 21, 22 above, 23, 24, and back of the jacket); Atelier Braumüller, Ethnological Museum, Munich (1, 2, 3, 18, and front of the jacket); Joerg Kirchner (6 below, 12); Dr. Hildesuse Gaertner (22 below); and ZFA Schmidt Tannwald (20 above)

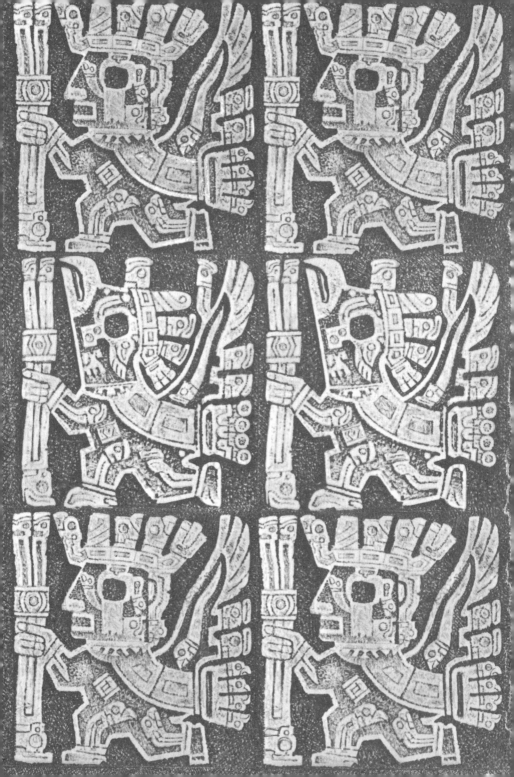